THE STORY

ADULT CURRICULUM
PARTICIPANT'S GUIDE

Resources for *The Story*

Books

The Story

The Story for Teens

The Story for Kids

The Story for Children, a Storybook Bible

The Heart of the Story (by Randy Frazee)

Exploring the Story (by Adam Barr)

Curriculum

The Story Adult Curriculum Participant's Guide and DVD

The Story Teen Curriculum DVD

The Story Elementary Curriculum CD-ROM

The Story Early Elementary Curriculum CD-ROM

The Story Preschool Curriculum CD-ROM

THE STORY

GETTING TO THE HEART OF GOD'S STORY

ADULT CURRICULUM
PARTICIPANT'S GUIDE
31 SESSIONS

RANDY FRAZEE

WITH KEVIN AND SHERRY HARNEY

ZONDERVAN

The Story Adult Curriculum Participant's Guide

Requests for information should be addressed to:

Zondervan, *Grand Rapids, Michigan 49530*

ISBN 978-0-310-32953-4

Interior production: Beth Shagene

Printed in the United States of America

11 12 13 14 15 16 /DCI/ 26 25 24 23 22 21 20 19 18 17 16 15 14 13 12 11 10 9 8 7 6 5 4

Contents

A Word from the Authors

As we journey through *The Story* in the days and weeks ahead, we will learn that heaven and earth are woven more closely together than we ever dreamed. All through the story of the Bible we see two parallel and beautiful dramas unfold.

There is the ***Upper Story***. God is real, he is present, and he is working on our behalf. Heaven is breaking into the world more than we recognize, and the story of God's seeking love, perpetual grace, and longing for relationship with ordinary people is breathtaking.

There is also the ***Lower Story***. We live on earth. We make mistakes, run from God, and resist his overtures of love. Sometimes we get so mired in the Lower Story that we fail to recognize God's presence breaking into our world. We forget that the God of heaven longs to have a growing relationship, a friendship, with us.

In the beginning of *The Story*, God walked with his first children in a beautiful garden ... in harmonious relationship. At the end of *The Story*, he will walk with us again, on streets of gold.

The question is: what will happen in the pages in between? As we walk through *The Story* together, we will see how the Upper Story and Lower Story are intertwined. All through history God has encountered, loved, sought, disciplined, and redeemed his children.

God is closer than we think.

Best of all, we can walk closely with him in every situation of life. He is near. He loves us. As we recognize how close the Upper Story and the Lower Story fit together, we will learn to experience God's love and grace as we walk through our days. We will never walk alone.

God wants to be with us; with you, with me. This is the refrain that rings true through *The Story*. As you read each chapter this will become clearer and more personal. On this journey, we will grow together and discover that the world is a smaller place than we knew.

God's story and our story are really one and the same.

The Heart of the Story and Our Story

Before the rise of the printing press in the sixteenth century, stories were passed down orally. The older people in a community shared the important stories of their history — all the principles and values of life woven within these gripping narratives. They shared these stories with each other, and with the next generation. It was a part of their culture ... their lives.

For the past few centuries, though, our communication primarily has been written — people sitting alone with a book open on their lap.

Now, however, with the explosive rise of technology (TV, movies, YouTube, and other visual communication tools), the world is returning to pictures and stories. We are once again becoming an oral culture. Indeed, many people learn best by hearing and telling stories.

With this in mind, we desire to capture this ancient/modern form of oral communication and weave it into your experience of *The Story*. To accomplish this, we have come up with five icons to help as you hear and tell the story. These simple pictures will put an image in your mind to help you remember the movements of God's story. They will also help as you tell your own story. Here are the images and the portion, or movement, of *The Story* that they represent:

PICTURE	PORTION OF THE STORY	PORTION OF THE BIBLE
	The Story of the *Garden*	Genesis 1–11
	The Story of *Israel*	Genesis 12–Malachi
	The Story of *Jesus*	Matthew–John (Gospels)
	The Story of the *Church*	Acts–Jude
NEW	The Story of a *New Garden*	Revelation

Over our thirty-one-week journey through *The Story,* the final question of each DVD Discussion will focus on one or more of these five movements, as indicated by the icon(s). Each one captures the Upper Story of God's work and also points to God's desire to encounter us in the Lower Story. Each session of your small group gathering will provide a brief time for your group to grow in your understanding of God's story as well as helping you learn to articulate his story and your own journey of faith. Please don't skip this important part of the study.

Our prayer is that each person who walks through the thirty-one sessions of *The Story Adult Curriculum Participant's Guide* will be able to do three things.

1. Identify the five movements listed on the previous page and how they shape *The Story.*
2. Articulate a short statement that captures the heart of each of the five sections of *The Story* (see below).
3. Connect the themes of God's story with your personal story. This will release you to naturally tell your story of faith in a way that intertwines with God's story.

Here are the five movements of *The Story.* As you become familiar with the themes and reflect on how they connect to God's story, they will help you articulate your own story of faith.

MOVEMENT 1: The Story of the *Garden* (Genesis 1–11)

In the Upper Story, God creates the Lower Story. His vision is to come down and be with us in a beautiful garden. The first two people reject God's vision and are escorted from paradise. Their decision introduces sin into the human race and keeps us from community with God. At this moment God gives a promise and launches a plan to get us back. The rest of the Bible is God's story of how he kept that promise and made it possible for us to enter a loving relationship with him.

MOVEMENT 2: The Story of *Israel* (Genesis 12–Malachi)

God builds a brand-new nation called Israel. Through this nation, he will reveal his presence, power, and plan to get us back. Every story of Israel will point to the first coming of Jesus — the One who will provide the way back to God.

MOVEMENT 3: The Story of *Jesus* (Matthew–John)

Jesus left the Upper Story to come down into our Lower Story to be with us and to provide the way for us to be made right with God. Through faith in Christ's work on the cross, we can now overturn Adam's choice and have a personal relationship with God.

MOVEMENT 4: The Story of the *Church* (Acts–Jude)

Everyone who comes into a relationship with God through faith in Christ belongs to the new community God is building called the church. The church is commissioned to be the presence of Christ in the Lower Story — telling his story by the way we live and the words we speak. Every story of the church points people to the second coming of Christ, when he will return to restore God's original vision.

MOVEMENT 5: The Story of a *New Garden* (Revelation)

God will one day create a new earth and a new garden and once again come down to be with us. All who placed their faith in Christ in this life will be eternal residents in the life to come.

May this journey through *The Story* inspire you to share God's story freely, because he wants to make his story your story.

Of Note

The quotes interspersed through this participant's guide are excerpts from *The Story Adult Curriculum* DVD, *The Story*, and materials developed by the authors in the writing of this study.

Creation:
The Beginning of Life as We Know It

People are the pinnacle of God's creative work,
and he is in relentless pursuit of a relationship with each of us.

Introduction

Sometimes in life we just need to get back to the basics. The bedrock. The foundation.

The story is told of the legendary Green Bay Packers coach, Vince Lombardi, starting the season by holding up a game ball and saying with slow clarity, "Gentlemen, this is a football." Similarly, to help his basketball players focus on the fundamentals, the great UCLA coach, John Wooden, would begin each season by teaching his team how to correctly put on their socks and tie their shoes. He believed there was a right way to do these simple tasks and that these acts impacted the rest of the game.

Both Lombardi and Wooden were very successful. Their insistence on putting "first things first" led their teams to many victories. Without a solid foundation, they both knew that the results would not have been as glorious.

Chapter 1 of *The Story* is God's version of "This is a football," or "This is how we put on our socks and tie our shoes." These opening pages provide the foundational building blocks. God is Creator and initiator. People are the crown of his creative activity. God wants to be in relationship with us. Though people messed up and embraced sin rather than their Creator, God loves us so desperately that he will do whatever it takes to build a bridge back to a relationship with us.

What a story! What a God!

Talk About It

What is a place in creation that really reveals God's glory to you and helps you feel close to him?

DVD Teaching Notes

As you watch the video segment for session 1, use the following outline to record anything that stands out to you.

God's Big Idea ... the point of the story is to be with us

The result of rejecting God's vision

The Upper and Lower Story perspectives of Cain and Abel's conflict

God's relentless efforts to get us back

DVD Discussion

1. When God looked at creation and declared it both "good" and "very good," what do you think he was trying to express?

   Randy suggested that God looks at you and says, "Looking at you is better than an ocean view ... or watching a sunrise." How does that make you feel?

> *What is the apple of God's eye?*
> *The magnum opus of his work?*
> *PEOPLE—US! Go figure, but it's true.*

2. Genesis 1:26–27 (*The Story*, pp. 2–3) says that we are made in the image of God. How do we, as people, actually reflect the image of God?

3. If you could take a walk with God in the perfect garden of paradise, just like you would with a friend, what would you ask him and why?

4. In a normal day, what gets in the way of you taking a walk with God and talking about what is on your heart?

5. Even though Adam and Eve began walking in perfect fellowship with their Maker, God still gave them freedom to reject this perfect life. What does this spiritual reality say about the power of the choices we make each day?

6. Adam and Eve made a choice to eat from the tree of knowledge of good and evil. They rejected God's vision for their lives and declared that they wanted to run their own universe and be their own god. How do you see that same sinful desire and behavior in our lives today and how does it influence our daily walk with God?

God's grand vision was to go on walks with his children; to be in their presence. God creates the Lower Story so he can come down from the Upper Story and do life with us.

7. If God truly loved Adam and Eve, why would he throw them out of the garden? Randy said that God's choice to drive Adam and Eve out of the garden was really an "act of grace." Do you agree or disagree with his statement and why do you feel this way?

8. What are ways to identify that we are about to enter into sinful and rebellious actions and how can we stop before we have crossed the line?

9. Read movement 1 of *The Story* (p. 10 of this participant's guide). What is the big theme of this first movement?

Closing Prayer

As you take time to pray, here are some ideas to get you started:

- Ask God to help you appreciate the beauty of his creation and to be a good steward and caretaker of the world he has made.
- Give praise to God for the people in your life who have revealed his grace, love, and presence to you.
- Pray for wisdom and discernment to recognize Satan's tactics as he tries to deceive you and the people you care about.

Between Sessions

Personal Reflections

Take time this week to meditate on the depth of God's love for human beings. Why would he keep pursuing us even after we have rebelled and rejected him? How can you express thanks for his seeking love? What can you do to celebrate the good news that God pursues you, even when you are not embracing his will and desires for you?

Personal Action

Take a walk outside and notice the beauty of what God has made. Look at the intricacies of a leaf or the expanse of the sky. Thank God for making this amazing world. As you walk, seek to talk to God as though you were two friends walking in a garden. Tell him about your life, feelings, joys, and fears. Ask him to help you learn to walk with him each and every day.

Read for Next Session

Take time before your next small group to read chapter 2 of *The Story*.

SESSION 2

God Builds a Nation

God will accomplish his plan and will in this world, but he often does it in ways we would not expect and through surprising people.

Introduction

Have you ever heard someone say, "The Lord works in mysterious ways"? This line is not from the Bible, but from the opening line of a hymn written in the eighteenth century by William Cowper. Nonetheless, people still use it because, well, the Lord *does* work in mysterious ways. The story of the Bible contains all sorts of times that God uses surprising people:

- Who will speak for God? Moses ... a man who hated public speaking.
- Who will lead God's people to military victory? Deborah ... a woman who was not trained as a warrior.
- Who will be a disciple of Jesus? Matthew ... a tax collector and a notorious sinner.
- Who will write half the books of the New Testament? Paul ... a man who had destroyed churches and killed Christians.

You get the picture. These are just four examples from a much longer list of surprising people God called and used. All through the pages of God's story we read about God working through the most unlikely of people.

As we are swept into the story of Abram and Sarai we begin to believe that God can use anyone. When this truth finds its way deep into our souls, we are filled with hope because we realize that God can do great things through anyone ... including us!

Talk About It

As we read *The Story* we discover that God is full of surprises. He rarely does things the way we would expect. Tell about a time God did something in your life (or the life of someone close to you) that was totally unexpected and surprising.

DVD Teaching Notes

As you watch the video segment for session 2, use the following outline to record anything that stands out to you.

God has a plan to get his people back

God picks an unlikely pair ... Abraham and Sarah give birth to a son, Isaac

Abraham is tested ... will he give God his best?

The significance of Mount Moriah in the Old and New Testaments

DVD Discussion

1. Many of the people God called to follow him and do great things had excuses or reasons they thought God should not use them. What are some of the common excuses people still use today when they want to get out of following God's leading for their life?

2. When God called Abram to follow him, there was a clear sense of partnership. God promised to do specific things and also called Abram to do his part (Genesis 12:1 – 5; *The Story*, p. 13). What was God's part and what was Abram's part in this great adventure?

3. What do you learn about Abraham and Sarah's faith from Hebrews 11:8 – 9 (a summary of *The Story*, pp. 13 – 20)?

4. Tell about an older person in your life who has been a model of faith and love for God. How have you seen their life impact the lives of others and yours?

> *"You think you're too old, you think you have missed your chance to do something big, something significant. That's the way we think in the Lower Story. But if we align our lives to God and what he's up to, some of our best years are still ahead of us."*

5. Abraham and Sarah were called by God and they followed him in faith. Tell about a time God called you to take a step of faith. How did you respond and how did that step of faith turn out?

6. Sarah did not think God was moving fast enough with the whole "nation building project." So, she decided to help God by giving her handmaid to Abraham to bear a child for her. Give some examples of ways we jump ahead of God's timing for our lives in an effort to "help" him.

Tell about a time that God said, "Wait," but you wanted to rush ahead. Why is it so hard to be patient and wait on God's will for our lives?

7. Abraham and Sarah chose to follow God by faith and trust that he would build a nation through them — and he did. What step of faith is God calling you to take now, but you are still waiting or even resisting? What can you do to take a trust-filled step and move forward in this area of your life?

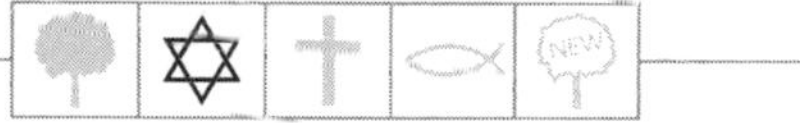

8. Read movement 2 of *The Story* (p. 11 of this participant's guide). What is the big theme of this second movement?

God is in the business of surprising us by using those who are weak, broken, outcast, questionable, and ordinary to accomplish his extraordinary plans in this world.

Closing Prayer

As you take time to pray, here are some ideas to get you started:

- Pray for strength to make the next step of faith that God is calling you to take.
- Ask God to grow your patience so you can wait on his will in each area of your life.
- Thank God for the older people he has placed in your life who have been a model of faith for you.

Between Sessions

Personal Reflections

God calls each of his children, at various times, to follow him in ways that are risky and demand faith. Look at your life and reflect honestly on these scenarios:

- When was a time God called me to step out in faith, but I missed the opportunity? (Confess this to God and receive his grace to let it go.)
- When was a time God invited me to take a bold step of faith and I followed with confidence? (Thank God for carrying you through that time.)
- Ask God to give you a sense of where he might be leading you in the future. Commit to follow him, no matter what anyone else might say or think.

Personal Action

Abraham took what was most precious to him and surrendered it to God. He would not hold back even his own son. Make a list of five to ten things that mean a great deal to you. One by one, offer them to God. If it is a person, surrender that loved one to the Lord. If it is a material thing, let God know that he has full access to it. If it is a talent or ability, tell God you will use it for him. Take everything and freely offer it back to the One who gave you all you have.

Read for Next Session

Take time before your next small group to read chapter 3 of *The Story.*

Joseph:
From Slave to Deputy Pharaoh

All of us naturally avoid times of struggle, pain, and hardship, but these moments in life might just be the tool God uses to accomplish his will in and through us.

Introduction

Pain avoidance is as natural as breathing. It is reflexive. Touch a hot plate and you will jerk your hand away without even thinking. If you see trouble down the road, you take an alternate route. It makes perfect sense to do what we can to avoid pain and struggle. But some of God's best work is done in the moments of life that feel more like a furnace than an afternoon sunbathing.

Sometimes a hard place is the right place for a person to meet God and become a useful instrument in the hand of the Master. This was true for Charles Colson, a brilliant political strategist and special counsel to President Richard Nixon in the 1970s. Though he was never actually prosecuted for any crime related to Watergate, he did plead guilty and was incarcerated for obstructing justice and spent time in prison.

It was this painful season that led Colson to seek the face of God and surrender his heart to Jesus Christ. In that low point God began to transform Colson into a new man. Since then he has led an amazing ministry called Prison Fellowship, founded the Wilberforce Forum, and impacted countless lives through his speaking, writing, and dynamic leadership.

Had Charles Colson never "gotten caught" and endured pain and struggle, he might never have encountered Jesus. He could testify that the hardest, darkest times are sometimes God's best times to capture our hearts and shape our lives.

Talk About It

If you have brothers or sisters, share about the general temperament among your siblings while growing up in your home.

DVD Teaching Notes

As you watch the video segment for session 3, use the following outline to record anything that stands out to you.

Meeting Joseph: favorite, dreamer, slave

Facing false accusations

Dream interpreter

A unique family reunion … God works all things out for good

DVD Discussion

1. From a human standpoint (the Lower Story), Joseph was in the worst place: abandoned by family, sold into slavery, cast into prison (Genesis 39:20 – 23; *The Story*, pp. 29 – 32). From a divine perspective (Upper Story), he was in the best place. How do you see God working in Joseph and showing blessing, even in the pain of these moments of his life?

2. In the darkest times of Joseph's life we read that "the LORD was with Joseph." How have you experienced the Lord being with you in the hard times of life? What are some of the signs that God is with us, even in the dark places?

3. Joseph waited two years in prison for someone to remember him and send help. Tell about a time you waited for months or years on an answer from the Lord. How did you make it through this long season of waiting?

You may be in a prison cell right now, either real or figuratively speaking, but if you align your life to God, your story isn't finished yet.

4. God has an amazing ability to bring good out of life's bad situations. Tell about a time when something hard and painful happened in your Lower Story, but later you saw God accomplish something wonderful in the Upper Story of his will.

5. At the end of chapter 3 of *The Story*, Joseph was reunited with his brothers twenty-two years after they sold him off as a slave. What strikes you about Joseph's attitude toward his brothers and the way he treats them? What does this teach us about the condition of his heart and the depth of his faith?

6. Joseph could have retaliated and gotten revenge on his brothers for all the wrong they had done to him. Instead, he provided for them and extended forgiveness. What makes it hard to forgive people who have intentionally wronged us? What can we do to forgive, even when it is difficult?

7. Charles Colson could say, "If I had not been caught and ended up in prison, I would never have become the man I am today." Joseph could say, "If my brothers had not turned on me, if Potiphar's wife had not falsely accused me, I would have never ended up meeting Pharaoh's servants in prison. I might have never become the king's right-hand man." Describe how your life would be different if you had never faced a specific time of challenge and struggle. Finish this statement: If I had not ______________________________, I would never have ____.

> *If we love God and align our lives to his Upper Story purposes, everything in our lives—the ups and downs, the mountaintops and the valleys, the highs and the hurts, the raises and the rejections, the good and bad—is all working together to accomplish his will.*

8. Romans 8:28 tells us, "In all things God works for the good of those who love him, who have been called according to his purpose." What is one situation in your life where you need to embrace and experience this truth? How can your small group pray for you as you walk through this season?

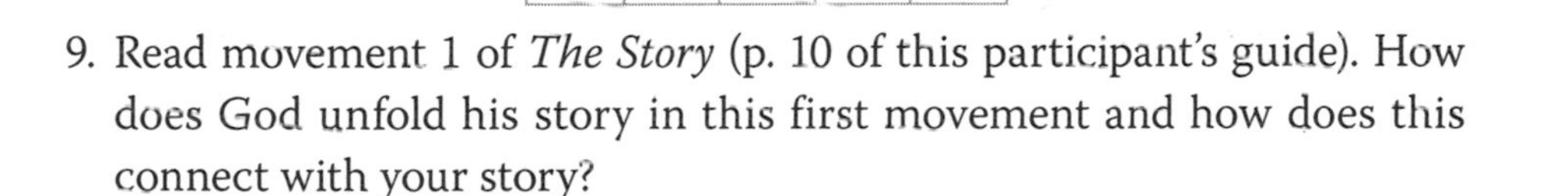

9. Read movement 1 of *The Story* (p. 10 of this participant's guide). How does God unfold his story in this first movement and how does this connect with your story?

Closing Prayer

As you take time to pray, here are some ideas to get you started:

- Pray for the families represented in your small group to be healthy and strong.
- Thank God for the hard times that have shaped your character and driven you closer to him.
- Pray for small group members who are traveling through a difficult season. Ask for God's comfort, but also for his work to be accomplished in their lives.

Between Sessions

Personal Reflections

Reflect back on your life. Where has God been at work shaping and forming you ... even in the hard times? Are there lessons God was seeking to teach you that you might have missed? Ask for eyes to see them and a heart to receive and learn. Are you facing something tough right now? If God wants to use this experience to grow you, ask for the courage to embrace it.

Personal Action

Forgiveness is one of life's hardest actions. When someone has really hurt us, it is extremely difficult to forgive. During the next week read Genesis 50:15 – 21, Matthew 6:9 – 15, and Matthew 18:21 – 35. Pray for the courage and strength you need to forgive those who have wronged you. Meditate on Romans 5:8 and ask God to help you understand the depth of his grace so that you can extend that grace to others.

Read for Next Session

Take time before your next small group to read chapter 4 of *The Story.*

SESSION 4

Deliverance

Be careful when you say "I could never" or "I would never."
God might just call you to do the very thing
you are sure would never show up on the radar of your life.

Introduction

All through *The Story* we will meet people who did not believe they had what it took to serve God. But, over and over again, God continued to use surprising people to accomplish his Upper Story plan down in this Lower Story world of ours.

He still does.

At seventeen years old, Joni Eareckson Tada unknowingly dove into shallow water and had her whole life change in a moment. She became a quadriplegic, no longer able to use her arms or legs. At that point she could have given up on life and rejected God. Instead she opened her heart wider and embarked on a path of passionate service. Through the pain, struggle, sense of inadequacy, and relentless challenges, Joni followed God's call on her life.

Over the next four decades this woman of faith learned to paint beautiful pictures by holding a brush in her teeth; she has written books, hosted a radio program, founded an organization to help people with disabilities, served on the Disability Advisory Committee for the U.S. State Department, and spoken at conferences around the world. Imagine what the world would have missed if Joni allowed her "limitation" to stop her from following the extraordinary call of God.

Talk About It

Tell about a person you know who has overcome obstacles and accomplished surprising things. What about that person encourages you?

DVD Teaching Notes

As you watch the video segment for session 4, use the following outline to record anything that stands out to you.

God is in control no matter what the circumstances

God always chooses the right point person: God's view of Moses

God's name

God will accomplish his plan

DVD Discussion

1. Tell about a time you were minding your own business, going through your normal Lower Story life, and God showed up, revealed himself, or spoke to you in some surprising way.

2. God is dramatically active in his people's deliverance — he is engaged, he cares (Exodus 3:1 – 10; *The Story*, pp. 45 – 46). Looking specifically at verses 7 – 10, what do you learn about God in the following areas:
   - What did God see, hear, and feel?
   - What did God say *he* would do?
   - What did God call *Moses* to do?

In the Lower Story it looked like Pharaoh was controlling the world. Not for one moment. The time has come for God to deliver Israel and get them back on the path toward his promise. It is time to once again reveal his name, his power, and his plan. He just needs the right point person.

3. How did Moses see himself and his abilities and how did God see him (Exodus 4:10 – 12; *The Story*, pp. 46 – 47)? Tell about a conversation you had with God that may have sounded something like the one Moses had in this passage.

4. While God saw Moses as the perfect person to face Pharaoh and speak the word of the Lord to the leader of Egypt, Moses saw himself as a political fugitive and a poor communicator who had no business facing the king. Give examples of how God can see us one way and we can see ourselves very differently. What can we do to increase our ability to see ourselves from God's perspective?

In the Lower Story Moses isn't qualified for such an important task. But in the Upper Story God sees Moses' weakness as the best channel for his strength. When Israel is successful in being freed from the Egyptian oppression, everyone will see God.

5. Randy suggested that the best thing we can do is to say yes to God, even when we do not feel adequate for the task ahead. Tell about a time when you dared to say yes and followed God, even when you were afraid. How did God show up and lead you?

6. God always was, is, and will be; he calls himself "I AM," the self-existent one (Exodus 3:14; *The Story*, p. 46). How can embracing the reality that the God we worship is the eternal "I AM" help you face the challenging moments of a normal day?

7. What is one area of your life where you tend to focus more on your limitations than God's ability to work through you? How can your group members pray for you and encourage you as you seek God's leading in this area?

8. How is Passover (Exodus 12:1 – 24; *The Story*, pp. 51 – 52) an ancient sign pointing to the death of Jesus on the cross as the final Lamb of God who will take away the sins of the world?

9. Read movement 2 of *The Story* (p. 11 of this participant's guide). How does God unfold his story in this second movement and how does this connect with your story?

Closing Prayer

As you take time to pray, here are some ideas to get you started:

- Thank God that he uses limited, ordinary, and even broken people to accomplish his purposes in this world.
- Ask God to help you see yourself through his eyes more than through your own eyes.
- Confess where you have refused to follow God out of fear and pray for greater courage in the future.

Between Sessions

Personal Reflections

We all have our "I could never" and "I hope God never asks me to ..." moments. Where are the places you tend to resist God's call? What things are you sure you could never do? As you honestly reflect on these questions, place them before the Lord, one by one. Admit your fear and resistance. Ask for new courage and boldness to follow God, even when you feel that you have nothing to offer or that your past disqualifies you. Commit to follow God, as best you can, no matter what he calls you to do.

Personal Action

Part of faith is taking action. If you feel prompted by God to sing in the church choir or play an instrument on the worship team, open your schedule and start practicing.

If you feel God calling you to the mission field, surrender and commit to follow. In addition, contact some mission organizations, talk to the missions leader in your church, go on a short-term mission trip, or take some other kind of action that will help you prepare.

You get the point. Surrender to the leading of the Lord, but also take action. God will do his part, but we need to do our part. God called Moses, but Moses had to head back to Egypt and stand before Pharaoh.

Read for Next Session

Take time before your next small group to read chapter 5 of *The Story*.

New Commands and a New Covenant

God gives his laws and commandments to free us, protect us, and show us his love ... not to take away our fun and ruin our lives.

Introduction

Every day that we get in a car and drive to work, school, church, the store, or anywhere else, we follow countless rules without even noticing. We respond, almost instinctively, to the "rules of the road."

We drive on the correct side of the road. We hit the brakes when we see a stop sign or red light. We are careful to go the right way on a one-way street. We merge when the sign tells us to merge. On a relatively short trip, a driver will make a hundred decisions based on the signs on the road and the rules they represent.

Following these simple driving instructions is not a recipe for ruining our trip or the joy of the open road. It is a way to make sure we stay alive! These rules protect us, direct us, and keep us (and others on the road) safe. Without them, a one-mile drive across town would be dangerous, chaotic, and potentially life-threatening.

Talk About It

When you were a child, how did you picture or imagine God? How has this changed through the years?

DVD Teaching Notes

As you watch the video segment for session 5, use the following outline to record anything that stands out to you.

Guidelines on how we should treat each other

Tabernacle accommodations

Atonement for sins

The God of the Upper Story wants to do life with the Lower Story

DVD Discussion

1. If we see God as a cosmic killjoy just waiting for people to do something wrong so he can catch and punish them, how will this impact our relationship with him?

2. The Ten Commandments are the basic "rules of the road" for how people are to relate to God and each other (Exodus 20:1 – 17; *The Story*, pp. 61 – 62). How would our lives and faith improve if we followed these commands (in action and in spirit)? What can we do to embrace and follow these commands more fully?

3. Randy unpacked the reality that God is seeking to come down and connect with his people ... with us! He said that three things need to happen for God to draw near to us in the Lower Story and experience his presence. Why is each of these so important?
   - There must be rules to guide how people relate to God and to each other
   - God will need a place to stay
   - Sin must be atoned for

The God of the Upper Story wants to come down and do life with us in the Lower Story. God is no longer going to be "up there" but "down here."

4. God no longer dwells in tents or temples; he lives in us (Acts 7:48 – 50; 1 Corinthians 6:19). How does recognizing that God dwells in us help connect his Upper Story to our Lower Story on a daily basis?

5. God showed his love for people and his desire to connect the Upper and Lower Story by moving into their neighborhood. He settled in, right in their midst. God is still seeking to connect with us on a deeply personal level. What are ways you experience the presence and care of God breaking into your daily life?

6. This chapter of *The Story* and Randy's lesson both reveal the third thing God had to do so that we could experience his presence in a personal way. The biggest obstacle of all needed to be overcome ... human sin. Sacrifices needed to be made so that human wrongs could be cleansed and covered over (atoned for). How does the sacrificial system found in *The Story* and the book of Leviticus pave the way for the final sacrifice that would wash away all sins forever (the death of Jesus on the cross)?

7. "Mad Cow Disease," as Randy called it, was an example of people trying to invent their own religion, to create their own way to God. How do people still do this today and how are the results just as disastrous?

8. God promised that his presence would be with the people and they would stand out in the world because of it. This is still true today. What are some ways Christians *should* stand out in our world? Name one area of your life in which you sense God is calling you to look different to the world because he is with you.

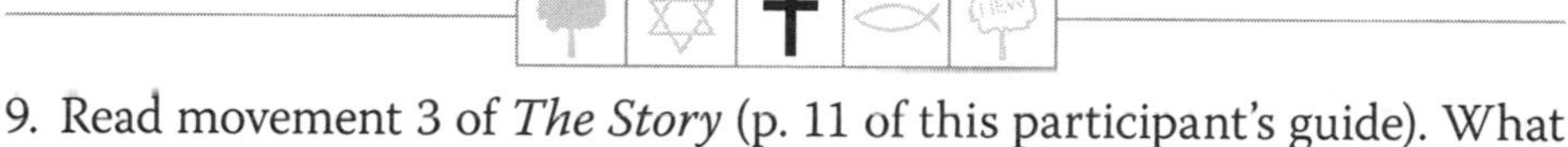

9. Read movement 3 of *The Story* (p. 11 of this participant's guide). What is the big theme of this third movement?

In God's community things are different. People are treated with full dignity and respect—no hurting, no hurling, no hoarding, no attacks, no withdrawing.

Closing Prayer

As you take time to pray, here are some ideas to get you started:

- Ask God to give you a clearer vision of who he is. Pray that it will not be tainted by false understandings and childish images, but shaped and informed by his Word.
- Welcome God, in growing measure, into your heart, home, church, and workplace.
- Thank Jesus for being the ultimate, complete, and final sacrifice for sin. Celebrate that you are made clean through his shed blood on the cross.

Between Sessions

Personal Reflections

Ask yourself: How am I doing when it comes to the three things God set in place so his story can connect more with my story? Am I seeking to do my part to ensure my relationship with God is as close as possible? Am I following his commands and direction? Am I seeking healthy relationships, loving others the way they would want to be loved? Do I invite God to dwell fully in my heart and life? How might I celebrate his presence in me and communicate with him more freely and more often? Do I live with an absolute, rock-solid confidence that all of my sins have been atoned for through Jesus' death on the cross and glorious resurrection?

Personal Action

Jesus took the helpful, life-giving information of the Ten Commandments and clarified it in the Sermon on the Mount. Read Matthew 5:17 – 48 this week. Let Jesus' teaching grow your understanding of how the commandments of God bring life and hope.

Read for Next Session

Take time before your next small group to read chapter 6 of *The Story.*

SESSION 6

Wandering

God has a great path planned for us
that includes joy and intimacy with him;
when we choose to take our own route
the journey is harder and takes longer.

Introduction

Have you ever missed an off-ramp on a highway and then realized it will be many miles before you can exit, turn around, and head back in the right direction? Driving all those unavoidable miles in the wrong direction feels frustrating, disappointing, and wasteful.

The people of Israel were traveling a relatively short distance after their deliverance from Egypt on the way to the Promised Land. With a small group it should have taken a matter of weeks. With more than a million people, it should have taken a month or two.

It ended up taking forty years!

Think about it. The trip should have taken a couple of months at the most. The people of God took two hundred and forty times longer to get to their destination than they needed to. That is a lot of wandering, a lot of wrong turns, a "we're running late" story of epic proportions.

This portion of *The Story*, this season of wanderings, contains some of the saddest and most painful accounts in all of the biblical narrative. It is a heart-wrenching read. But it wakes us up to the reality that God continues to be with his people, even when they are running the other direction and walking in circles ... in a desert.

Talk About It

Tell a story about a time you got lost on a drive or a hike. Where did things go wrong and how did you finally find your way home?

DVD Teaching Notes

As you watch the video segment for session 6, use the following outline to record anything that stands out to you.

Exploration of the land of milk and honey

Conflicting reports

A forty-year detour

The ultimate GPS system

DVD Discussion

1. Describe some of the ways that God might help us recalculate our life direction and get back on track when we are wandering.

2. All through this chapter of *The Story* God disciplines the people (sometimes quite strongly) to get them back on course. What are the values of being disciplined by one who loves us and wants the best for us?

> *Our life is like a road trip. God wants to lead us every step of the way with his GPS. God sees the picture from the Upper Story and wants the best for us. He wants us to make it to the final destination and to enjoy the journey.*

3. Randy mentioned that there were no less than ten outbreaks of "juvenile behavior" by the people of Israel during their desert wanderings. How can Christians today be like this — complaining, grumbling, and rebelling against God's leading and plan? Give an example of how you can fall into this pattern if you are not careful.

4. Ten of the men who spied out the land let their minds and eyes focus on the obstacles (Numbers 13:26 – 33; *The Story*, p. 75). What are ways we can be frozen by fear and fixate on the obstacles rather than the God who can help us overcome them?

5. How have you seen the sins of one generation poison and damage those who came after them? And conversely, how have you seen good choices and spiritual maturity be passed on as a blessing to the next generation?

We need to be reminded that whatever choice we make, our lives impact others. They will experience the blessings of our good decisions and they will experience the pain of our destructive choices.

6. What is one way you are seeking to pass on a healthy and positive legacy to the next generation? How can your group members pray as you seek to be a blessing to children, grandchildren, or the young people you influence?

7. Randy talked about the vision God has for his children to be responsive to his leading. When God says to go left or right, we turn and go. When he says stop, we hit the brakes. What kinds of things can get in the way of us responding to God's clear direction?

8. What will help us hear and respond more quickly when the Lord is seeking to lead us? What is one area of your life where you would like to be more responsive to God's leading and how can your group members support you in this?

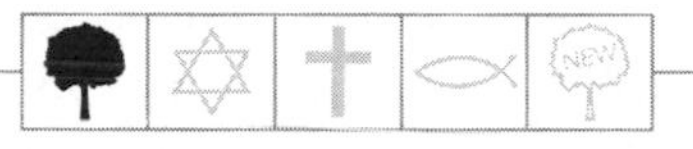

9. Read movement 1 of *The Story* (p. 10 of this participant's guide). How have you experienced God pursuing you and seeking to build a strong relationship with you?

church

1. Scriptural
2. Is it practical – purpose
3. Holy Spirit prompting

Closing Prayer

As you take time to pray, here are some ideas to get you started:

- Thank God for his loving discipline and invite him to help you stay on his course for your life.
- Confess where you have wandered from God's plan for your life and ask him to help you recalculate.
- Pray for a mature heart and spirit that does not complain, grumble, and whine when things do not go your way.

Between Sessions

Personal Reflections

Reflect on any ways your life has gotten off course. Ask God to help you recalculate and get back on the right path. Confess where you have been stubborn and rebellious, and think deeply of the grace you have received in Jesus. Then, identify ways you need to change your actions, attitudes, and motives to bring them in line with God's will for you.

Personal Action

One of the best things we can do is listen to people of wisdom and faith. In chapter 6 of *The Story*, Joshua and Caleb came back from their exploration of the land and gave wise counsel. Unfortunately, the people did not listen to them. Find one or two wise men or women of faith that know you well and ask for their insight and perspective on your life. Share how you are seeking to follow God and where you feel you are wandering off course. Invite their wisdom and prayerfully listen to them. Consider asking if they will meet with you on a regular basis to be a sounding board as you seek to walk with Jesus.

Read for Next Session

Take time before your next small group to read chapter 7 of *The Story.*

SESSION 7

The Battle Begins

This might surprise you,
but following God involves engaging
in an ongoing series of battles
to live in his will and walk in his ways ...
this will always be part of our story.

Introduction

Have you ever watched a documentary on how salmon swim upstream to spawn? These fish swim with all their might, against a strong current. They literally launch themselves up waterfalls and over jagged rocks. An irresistible force drives them upward and onward. It is inspiring to watch.

But some of the salmon get tired. In their exhaustion they stop swimming and immediately are swept backward ... downstream. The current gets the best of them and they give up.

Following God's will in this world can be a lot like being a salmon swimming upstream. God calls us to fight against the cultural current every day of our lives! It is a battle, a war, and daily challenge to keep living for God in a world where the flow is diametrically opposed to God's will and ways.

We have a choice. Swim with all our might and keep fighting and pressing on. Or, give up and find ourselves floating back downstream. We make this choice many times each day.

Talk About It

Can you think of a time in your life when you were faced with an overwhelming challenge that you needed to confront? What was it and how did you respond?

DVD Teaching Notes

As you watch the video segment for session 7, use the following outline to record anything that stands out to you.

God instructs Joshua: "Be strong and courageous"

Committing to be a people of the Word

Growing as a people of prayer

Proud to be a people identified with God

DVD Discussion

1. What did God call his people to do as they got ready to enter the Promised Land (Joshua 1:1 – 11; *The Story*, pp. 89 – 90)?

2. The first time spies were sent into the land, twelve of them went. Only two gave a good report; the other ten were so negative that they convinced the people of Israel the rewards weren't worth the risk. Four decades later, Joshua sent a team of only two into the land. Randy said, "Committees seldom make courageous decisions." Discuss the value of following a couple of bold leaders rather than a committee when it comes to those moments when we need to move forward quickly and with courage.

3. Just like the people of Israel, we sometimes are fearful of challenges and don't want to deal with them. What challenge in your life have you put on the back burner, but you know it is time to face it and deal with it? How can your group members pray for you, cheer you on, and keep you accountable in this process?

In the Lower Story the giants are bigger than the Israelites. In the Upper Story God is bigger than the giants.

4. How does consistent and faith-filled reading of the Bible (God's Story) help us remain strong and courageous as we swim upstream against the currents of this world?

   What are your personal habits and commitments when it comes to Bible study? How can your group members encourage you to grow in your love for God's Word?

> *Keep this Book of the Law always on your lips; meditate on it day and night, so that you may be careful to do everything written in it. Then you will be prosperous and successful.*
> *(Joshua 1:8;* The Story, *p. 89)*

5. Joshua read the words of God's story to all the people: children, teens, and the adults. What are ways we can help the children and young people in our lives grow in their knowledge of and love for the Bible? How can this be done in both our homes and churches?

6. Chapter 7 of *The Story* teaches us that we should always talk with God to make sure he is going before us and that we are not heading off on our own. Why is it so important to pray, listen to God, and follow his leading when we make life decisions? What are some of the possible

consequences if we forget to do this? What area of your life do you need to commit to more prayer and listening?

7. Baptism is an outward sign of our identification with God. What is the meaning of baptism and why is this public celebration so important and powerful? Have a few people share their baptism stories.

8. When Christians live in a world that flows so strongly against the desires and heart of God, we often are identified as believers simply by the way we live. Name some actions and attitudes that show the world we are followers of Jesus.

Rick Warren

9. Read movement 2 of *The Story* (p. 11 of this participant's guide). How have you seen God seeking to reveal his presence, power, and plan in your life?

impulse decision

peace,

Closing Prayer

As you take time to pray, here are some ideas to get you started:

- Pray for a renewed and deeper love for God's Word and a commitment to read and study it daily.
- Ask God to help you communicate more often and with greater intimacy as you speak with him in prayer.
- Pray that your group members would grow more bold and courageous and be ready to face any challenge or battle that God places before them.

Between Sessions

Personal Reflections

Think through the three areas of preparation for battle that Randy discusses from chapter 7 of *The Story*:

- How can I go deeper into God's Word and follow it with greater passion in my daily life?
- What steps can I take to make more space for conversation with God in my normal day, especially when I am facing battles?
- When people look at me, in a normal day, do they see that I am a follower of Jesus? What can I do to live and think in ways that will identify me more closely with the Savior?

Personal Action

In the course of reading chapter 7 of *The Story* and meeting with your group, God might have brought to your attention an area of your life where you have given in and stopped swimming against the current of our world. It is not that you don't care, but you are being swept downstream in the wrong direction. If you felt such a conviction, make a commitment to take specific steps to follow God's will, resist temptation, and begin your battle against this particular area of sin or apathy. Find a friend who will pray for you and keep you accountable to keep up the good fight.

Read for Next Session

Take time before your next small group to read chapter 8 of *The Story*.

SESSION 8

A Few Good Men ... and Women

God is in the business of bringing sinful people back into relationship with him; sometimes to accomplish this goal, he calls on surprising and unexpected people to help in the process.

Introduction

Albert Einstein once said that insanity is "doing the same thing over and over again and expecting different results." If we use this definition, then the people of Israel look pretty crazy in this chapter of *The Story*. In the time of the Judges the people of God went through the same cycle over and over again. Each time they rebelled and turned away from God they would face the same results: a foreign army would invade and they would end up an oppressed, occupied, and broken nation.

You would think that after living through this cycle two or three times they would have caught on. But this chapter of *The Story* makes clear that they did not learn from past experience. Every time they ended up oppressed and abandoned, they were shocked!

As we read these Bible accounts, it would be easy to wag a finger at our ancestors of the faith. But when we look into a mirror and examine our own lives, we just might see ourselves acting a lot like the people of Israel, wallowing in the same cycle of sin month after month and year after year.

Talk About It

If you could talk with an angel and have one "why" question answered, what would you ask?

DVD Teaching Notes

As you watch the video segment for session 8, use the following outline to record anything that stands out to you.

Gideon asks the "why" question

The truthful answer to the "why" question

Israel's cycle

Gideon's victory, God's way

DVD Discussion

1. Through *The Story* we have discovered that God loves to use surprising people to accomplish his will. As you read about Deborah, Gideon, and Samson in this chapter of *The Story*, how is each of them a surprising choice to be a leader for God?

> *God often selects the most unlikely candidate to accomplish his Upper Story plan. Why? So when it is accomplished everyone will know it was God. Then they will turn to him.*

2. Contrast how God saw Gideon with how Gideon saw himself (Judges 6:11 – 16; *The Story*, p. 108). How does this breathe hope into our hearts in the moments we feel God could never do great things through us?

3. In the continual cycle that occurs in the time of the Judges, God's people kept embracing the sins, religion, and behaviors of those who lived in the land before they conquered it. In what ways do Christians today embrace the sin, practices, and culture of our day and end up sinning and feeling distant from God?

How can we identify the temptation to be conformed to the world's sinful ways and avoid this pitfall?

4. One of the recurring themes in this chapter of *The Story* is that a new generation would rise up that did not know God and what he had done for his people in the past. When they forgot, they wandered. This same tragic thing can happen in our generation. What practical things can we do in our homes and in the church to help the next generation know and remember what God has done in the past so they will hold on to him in the future?

5. There seems to be consequences when we refuse to follow God's way. Why do you think we continue to repeat the same sin patterns even though we know the outcome will not be good?

6. Where would you be today if God had never allowed his discipline to wake you up to the reality of sin and drive you into his arms?

As Christians, we get ourselves into all sorts of trouble because we want to live life the way we want, not God's way. In the Lower Story we think that God has abandoned us. But in the Upper Story God is waiting for us to return to him. His arms are wide open.

7. How did God strengthen Gideon and help him press through his fears as he faced the mighty armies of Midian? How does God do this same thing today when we feel inadequate and fearful?

8. Have you faced a situation when the odds were against you, and others said, "No way!" but you held God's hand and pressed on? How did the situation turn out and how was God glorified?

   What area in your life is God presently trying to get you to the place where you embrace the fact that he is enough?

---

9. Read movement 3 of *The Story* (p. 11 of this participant's guide). How does God unfold his story in this third movement and how does this connect with your story?

Closing Prayer

As you take time to pray, here are some ideas to get you started:

- Confess the tendency we have to forget the great things God has done in the past. Ask him to help you remember his faithfulness each day.
- Thank God that when his people repent and cry out for help, he always sends a deliverer. Give special praise that Jesus came as the One who offers final and absolute deliverance.
- Tell God that you are ready to follow him and seek to do his will, even when you feel inadequate for the task.

Between Sessions

Personal Reflections

Are there any patterns of rebellion and struggle in your life? What does your personal life pattern look like when it comes to sin and wandering from God? What is one step you can take to begin to break that pattern?

Personal Action

Read and meditate on Moses' song found in Deuteronomy 32. Let the message of this song move deep into your soul. You might even want to write it down and put it somewhere where you will see it on a regular basis. If you are musical, you might want to set it to music. Let the message of this short song remind you of God's goodness and our human temptation to fall back into the same sins over and over.

Read for Next Session

Take time before your next small group to read chapter 9 of *The Story*.

SESSION 9

The Faith of a Foreign Woman

When things seem hopeless and life feels meaningless, God might just be getting ready to do some of his best work.

Introduction

In the iconic 1990s comedy *Dumb and Dumber*, one of the main characters, Lloyd Christmas, falls for a woman named Mary. At a dramatic moment he finally asks her if there is any chance they will end up together. Here is their brief dialogue:

Lloyd: What are my chances?

Mary: Not good.

The music comes to an abrupt stop and there is an awkward pause ...

Lloyd: You mean "not good" like one in a hundred?

Mary: I'd say more like one out of a million.

Another pause as Lloyd processes this information ... then he speaks with exuberance.

Lloyd: So you're telling me there's a chance ... yah!

What makes this so humorous is that everyone knows there is no chance in the world ... except Lloyd. He is a hopeless optimist.

As we continue through *The Story* we encounter time after time when things seem hopeless and impossible. From a Lower Story perspective we look and say, "This is a one-in-a-million chance ... really no chance at all." Then, beyond all reason, God speaks from the Upper Story and tells us there really is a chance!

Talk About It

Tell about a time God showed up and did something surprising and unexpected in a seemingly hopeless situation that you (or someone you know) faced.

DVD Teaching Notes

As you watch the video segment for session 9, use the following outline to record anything that stands out to you.

Ruth's faithfulness to Naomi

Ruth's hard work and noble character

Boaz: the kinsman-redeemer

Baby Obed: a reminder that God has been at work through the whole story

DVD Discussion

1. As you read chapter 9 of *The Story*, what were some of the losses that Naomi and Ruth faced? How did each of them respond to these painful experiences?

2. Naomi was a person of faith, but she also questioned God and was deeply honest about her struggles (Ruth 1:19 – 21; *The Story*, p. 122). In what ways did Naomi's losses impact how she viewed God and his work in her life?

   Tell about a time you were honest with God about your pain and hurt. As you look back on that episode, what have you learned about God's presence and faithfulness?

3. Boaz was a man of amazing character and wisdom (Ruth 2 – 3; *The Story*, pp. 123 – 126). What can we learn from Boaz's interactions with his workers, including Ruth?

4. Throughout chapter 9 of *The Story* we get glimpses into Ruth's character as well. What are some of the exemplary aspects of her heart, attitudes, and behavior? How might Ruth be a role model for people today?

5. Near the end of chapter 9 of *The Story* (Ruth 4:1 – 10), Boaz offers another family member the opportunity to pay for and redeem the land of Naomi's dead husband and his two sons. When this other family member realizes it will cost him a great deal and gain him nothing financially, he declines. At this point, Boaz pays for all the property and allows the name of Elimelech (Naomi's husband) to be remembered. Give examples of things God calls Christians to do that cost us a great deal and do not pay off much (in this life or the eyes of the world).

6. How did Jesus' life model service and sacrifice for people who really had nothing with which to pay him back?

What has Jesus given you that you could never truly pay back? How can we express gratitude for his amazing generosity?

Jesus is the ultimate Kinsman-Redeemer.

7. When you think of how Naomi's life went from Mara (bitter) to Naomi (beautiful), what were the ways God extended grace to this faithful woman? Who needs you to come alongside of them to remind them that they are loved (or beautiful) and what is one action you can take this week to extend God's grace to this person?

Right now your story might seem a little hopeless and bitter to the taste. But remember, if you love God and align your life to his purposes you will discover that God is working it all out for the good. Wait patiently and God will unfold his good plan!

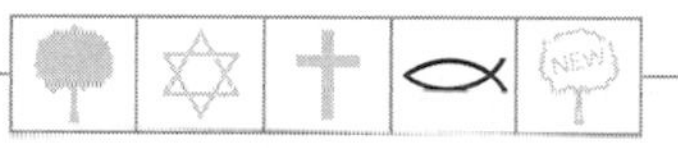

8. Read movement 4 of *The Story* (p. 11 of this participant's guide). What is the big theme of this movement?

Closing Prayer

As you take time to pray, here are some ideas to get you started:

- Pray for the people you love and care about who are going through a hard time in life right now.
- Thank God that he is in control of the Upper Story even when times seem hopeless. Ask him to give you strength to remain faithful when times are tough. Praise God that he is behind the scenes leading and guiding you.
- Ask God to help you be like Boaz and grow as a person who extends the gracious care of God to those who are often forgotten.

Between Sessions

Personal Reflections

Reflect on some of the main characters in this amazing narrative and pray for your life to reflect some of the same God-honoring attitudes and behavior:

- *Naomi*: Learn from her example of faith even in the hard times, from her care for her daughters-in-law, and from her honesty about her pain and loss.
- *Ruth*: Learn from her devotion to Naomi, from her commitment to work hard, and from her trust in God.
- *Boaz*: Learn from his compassion to a person in need, from his generosity, and from his integrity.

Personal Action

Be a Boaz. He showed compassion to a person in need. Think through the coming week and identify one or two acts of compassion and generosity you can extend to a person who is hurting, marginalized, and in need.

Read for Next Session

Take time before your next small group to read chapter 10 of *The Story.*

SESSION 10

Standing Tall, Falling Hard

Keeping up with the Joneses is never a good idea,
but it is particularly dangerous
when the Joneses are a bad example!

Introduction

In the early 1800s Charles Caleb Colton coined the phrase, "Imitation is the sincerest form of flattery." Of course, he was simply observing what had been part of human nature for all history. People tend to do what the people around them are doing ... for better or for worse!

Companies spend millions of dollars on marketing trying to figure out how to get more women to buy their perfume, more kids to purchase their brand of soft drink, more people to think of their restaurant when they are hungry — how to get every member of the human family to all decide to do the same thing and still see themselves as unique.

It is the human need to fit in that makes parents nervous when their kids are growing up. We want our sons and daughters around kids who make good choices because we know that when our kids make friends they will start dressing like them, talking like them, and thinking like them before we know it. For this same reason a parent's blood runs cold when a daughter or son starts hanging out with a group of kids who are making poor and dangerous decisions.

Our heavenly Father knows us. He understands the human tendency to imitate what we see and is concerned that we follow his example. Sadly, we are often enticed to follow the example of our culture instead.

Talk About It

Describe yourself as a middle schooler. What were you into, what styles did you wear, what music did you like, and who were the big influences in your life?

DVD Teaching Notes

As you watch the video segment for session 10, use the following outline to record anything that stands out to you.

God hears Hannah's cry: Samuel is born

The people of Israel want to be like all the other nations

Israel's first king, Saul

Samuel tells Saul that God has rejected him as king

DVD Discussion

1. First Samuel 1 (*The Story*, pp. 129 – 131) tells Hannah's heartbreaking account of barrenness and how her prayer for a child is finally answered. What strikes you about Hannah's character and faith?

> *God opens the womb of Hannah and provides her with the child she longed for in the Lower Story. God loves to do stuff like that for us. She appropriately names him "Samuel," which in Hebrew means "heard from God."*

2. What does Eli teach Samuel about listening to God (1 Samuel 3:1 – 10; *The Story*, pp. 131 – 132)? What can we learn about communicating with God as we see Samuel's story unfold?

3. According to 1 Samuel 8 (*The Story*, pp. 135 – 136), how does Samuel feel about the leaders of Israel's request to give them a king so they can be like all the other nations? How does God feel about it?

> *God is not looking for people who want to be like everyone else; he is looking for people who want to be like Christ.*

4. How does Samuel's description of the consequences of having an earthly king instead of a heavenly King parallel the actions of those who govern in our modern world today?

5. God's Upper Story plan is for him alone to rule as King over his people. In the Lower Story, the people insist on having an earthly king as their ruler. God gives in to their request. Do you believe God still allows us to have our way (on occasion) even if it is not his perfect will for us? If so, give an example of what this can look like.

6. Saul does not follow God's instructions, which leads to Samuel telling him that he will lose his throne because God has rejected him as king. Randy points out that one of Saul's big mistakes was distorting and misrepresenting God as cruel and greedy rather than showing he is just and holy. Why is God so concerned about his people giving an accurate portrayal of who he is? What can we do to present God to the world with greater clarity and accuracy?

7. God's desire is to reveal his presence, power, and plan to the world and thus restore people's relationship with him. How do you see God do each of these in this chapter of *The Story*:
   - Reveal his *presence*
   - Display his *power*
   - Execute his *plan* to get us back

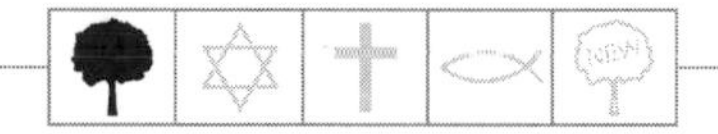

8. Read movement 1 of *The Story* (p. 10 of this participant's guide). If one of your group members has memorized this short statement that describes the heartbeat of the first movement, allow them to quote it and tell about what God taught them as they committed this statement to memory.

Closing Prayer

As you take time to pray, here are some ideas to get you started:

- Ask God to help you see where you are being conformed to the world and pray for strength to follow his plan for your life instead.
- Confess where you are tempted to imitate the world or poor examples and pray that you will experience both God's grace and power to change.
- Ask for the courage you need to follow God's direction in your life. Pray that you will not come up with your own version of the instructions, but will stick with his.

Between Sessions

Personal Reflections

The human capacity to self-deceive and rationalize sin is staggering. This pattern cost Saul his kingship. Reflect this week on any patterns in your life where you tend to rationalize sin. If God convicts you of an area of your life where this is happening, honestly confess it and ask for his strength to change.

Personal Action

Just like the people of Israel in Samuel's day and junior high school kids today, we can be prone to imitate and follow bad examples. Think through your behaviors, practices, shopping patterns, clothing choices, language, hobbies ... anything you might do because someone else does it. If you identify something that is unhealthy, ungodly, or offensive, commit to ending that behavior!

Read for Next Session

Take time before your next small group to read chapter 11 of *The Story.*

SESSION 11

From Shepherd to King

You really can't judge a book by its cover,
but when you open it and start reading
you will learn the real story.

Introduction

Our world is not just concerned about outward appearance ... we are pathologically obsessed with how we look.

People spend untold amounts of money on just the right clothes, the perfect pair of shoes, sports jerseys of their favorite team, hairstyles, jewelry, the right car, and all sorts of other things that will help us improve our appearance. Some people will do almost anything to "look right" and "fit in," to the point of paying for surgeries that tuck, lift, flatten, and even enhance body features.

In youth culture the trends and styles seem to change faster and faster, and teenagers who can't stay current are considered "out of it." This obsession is even pressing down into children's styles and appearance.

We might think this fixation on outward appearance is the product of our modern world or birthed in the back rooms of the marketing machine of Madison Avenue. The truth is: the human tendency to focus on outward appearance goes all the way back to the ancient world of the Bible. It is as old as human history.

Talk About It

Tell about a time you met someone and made a snap judgment about him or her, only to later learn that you were way off.

DVD Teaching Notes

As you watch the video segment for session 11, use the following outline to record anything that stands out to you.

God looks at David and sees a king (no one else saw David this way)

Fourteen years between anointing and inauguration ... God is working

God takes note of David's heart

How David's story points to God's Upper Story ... God is seeking to get us back

DVD Discussion

1. In this chapter of *The Story*, many different people think they have David figured out. How did each of these people view David when they looked at him?
   - His father, Jesse (1 Samuel 16:8 – 12; *The Story*, pp. 145 – 146)
   - The prophet Samuel (1 Samuel 16:7 – 13; *The Story*, pp. 145 – 146)
   - His brother, Eliab (1 Samuel 17:28; *The Story*, p. 148)
   - King Saul (1 Samuel 17:33 – 39; *The Story*, pp. 148 – 149)
   - Goliath (1 Samuel 17:41 – 44; *The Story*, p. 149)

2. God saw David quite differently from everyone else. In light of this chapter of *The Story*, how did God see David?

David might have been considered a runt on the outside, but God examined his heart on the inside and beheld a giant.

3. This chapter includes two powerful prayers of David: one from Psalm 59 (*The Story*, p. 152) and another from 2 Samuel 22:1 – 7, 47; Psalm 18 (*The Story*, pp. 154 – 155). What do you learn about David's heart from these honest, passionate cries to God?

4. Randy said, "God put David through spiritual boot camp to chisel him and refine him into the kind of man who truly trusted God." Tell about a time God sent you to spiritual boot camp (or has presently enrolled you). How did God use this time to refine, strengthen, and grow you?

5. David had to wait fourteen years between being anointed and actually sitting on the throne. Have you ever had a lengthy wait to receive something you felt God had planned for your life? What kept you hopeful during the wait?

6. Reading *The Story* we discover that David had his share of struggles and sins. But through it all he was a man whose heart sought after God. What are the things that tend to distract your heart and pull it away from God? What can we do to keep our hearts focused on God and growing more in love with him?

7. In this session's DVD segment Randy made a provocative statement: "God can use our disobedient lives as effectively as he uses our obedient lives in the Lower Story to work out his Upper Story plans." Do you agree with this statement? Give an example from the Bible that supports what Randy says.

8. *The Story* recounts that many of God's children had long seasons of waiting (often in tough times and sometimes in a desert). How can God use times of waiting and challenging seasons of life to prepare us for greater things in our future?

If you are in a time of waiting on the Lord right now, what can you do to remain faithful to God during this season? How can your group members pray for you and support you while you are in this waiting season?

> *There is a lot going on in David's story that points us to God's Upper Story plan to get us back. David was referred to as God's Anointed One. Those two words in English are one word in Hebrew—"Messiah." David was the Messiah in the Lower Story. His righteous reign points us to the Messiah in the Upper Story.*

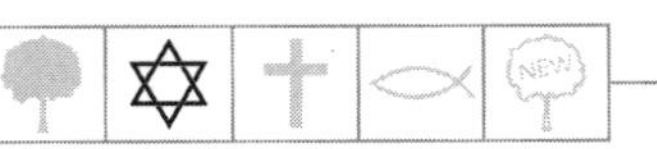

9. Read movement 2 of *The Story* (p. 11 of this participant's guide). If one of your group members has memorized this short statement that describes the heartbeat of the second movement, allow them to quote it and tell about what God taught them as they committed this statement to memory.

Closing Prayer

As you take time to pray, here are some ideas to get you started:

- Ask God to teach you to look beyond outward appearances (in yourself and in others).
- Pray for people you know who are in a challenging time of waiting. Ask God to carry them through and pray for wisdom to know how you can support or encourage them.
- Invite God to do what it would take to refine you and prepare you to be used by him in greater ways.

Between Sessions

Personal Reflections

Think about a time of waiting in your life, when you felt that God was refining you. Reflect on the lessons you learned while you waited. Have you carried them forward into the present day? Were there any lessons you missed that God still wants to teach you?

Personal Action

In our personal deserts and seasons of waiting, we need to remember that God is with us. But we can also take comfort in knowing that God's people are walking with us too. Think about a family member or friend who is in the midst of a hard time. Pray for them. Ask God to use you as a conduit of his love, a visible reminder that he is with them, caring for them. And ask them how you might come alongside to offer care and support.

Read for Next Session

Take time before your next small group to read chapter 12 of *The Story*.

SESSION 12

The Trials of a King

Sin costs us and other people ...
more than we ever dream.

Introduction

Did you ever play with dominos as a kid? And did you ever carefully stand a large number of them one next to the other on a hard surface, until you had a major configuration of dominos all standing at attention like little soldiers? Then, with trembling finger, you gently pushed one over and delighted as a chain reaction—a "domino effect"—occurred and all the tiles tumbled. The sensation is glorious. Even the sound of falling dominos brings a strange satisfaction.

This is the whole point of meticulously setting up a domino display. For some people, experiencing a line of dominos falling has become a life obsession. Presently the world record for domino tiles lined up and pushed over is an astounding 4,234,027.

In chapter 12 of *The Story* we read about another domino effect, one having to do with sin. When we commit a sin, our one action can begin a chain reaction of other sins ... click, click, click ... until down we fall.

We also see a domino effect as one person sins and those around them are affected. We never sin in isolation. Our choices impact the people around us. We are standing so close to them that when we fall, our lives bump theirs, and often they go down with us.

Talk About It

Tell about a time in your childhood when you made a sinful choice and it led to a series of other sins.

DVD Teaching Notes

As you watch the video segment for session 12, use the following outline to record anything that stands out to you.

King David's successful reign

David's pivotal life shift: enter Bathsheba

David's cover-up exposed

King David's response and restoration

DVD Discussion

1. As chapter 12 of *The Story* begins (2 Samuel 11; *The Story*, pp. 161 – 162), we see David enter into sin and begin a domino effect of other sins that followed. Identify each of David's sins and how it led to another sinful choice or action in his life.

2. David's sins did not just affect him but others around him. Note the effects on the following:
   - Bathsheba
   - Uriah
   - The prophet Nathan
   - The military commander Joab
   - Other soldiers under Joab's command
   - The baby conceived by Bathsheba
   - Other people in David's life

3. Once Uriah was dead, David seemed to think he had gotten away with his coveting, adultery, lying, and murder. But when Nathan confronted him, David realized that God knew everything. What are some of the ways we can deceive ourselves into thinking we have covered our tracks and hidden our sins (from ourselves, others, and even God)?

4. King Saul (when confronted by Samuel the prophet) did not admit his sin, repent, and really seek forgiveness ... he made excuses. That is why God rejected him. How is David's response to facing the reality of his sinfulness different from Saul's (2 Samuel 12; *The Story*, pp. 162 – 163)?

5. God forgave David, but there were still consequences to his sinful actions. What were some of the consequences David faced immediately and over the long term because of his sinful choices?

Why is it important that we walk in God's grace but still realize we might face very real consequences of our sins?

Just because we admit that we have done the wrong thing and even make it right doesn't mean the consequences will go away.

6. What do we learn about the holiness and heart of God when we consider Nathan's interactions with David?

7. If you could have asked David at the end of his life, "What advice and insight would you give me about temptation and sin?" what might David say to you if you are presently dabbling in sin?

8. Randy pointed out that David's life, even with his falls and frailties, still pointed people to God. How can God use our lives — the good and bad — to show his presence, love, and grace to the people around us?

There were grave consequences for David's actions, but because he did the right thing, his relationships were restored — most importantly, his relationship with God.

9. Read movement 3 of *The Story* (p. 11 of this participant's guide). How has the death and resurrection of Jesus become a bridge for you to cross and enter a more intimate relationship with God?

Closing Prayer

As you take time to pray, here are some ideas to get you started:

- Pray for eyes to see the domino effect of your sins *before* you commit them. Ask God for an awareness of the cost to you and others so that you will desire holiness and not live with the collateral damage of sin.
- Pray that God will place people in your life who love you enough to confront you about your sins. Invite the Holy Spirit to soften your heart so that you will humbly receive their words of conviction and correction.
- Thank God that the grace of Jesus is always sufficient to cover all of our sins.

Between Sessions

Personal Reflections

Ask yourself: How do I respond when people confront or correct me? Am I like Saul, covering my tracks? Or am I like David, listening, receiving, and repenting?

Personal Action

This is a big and bold action challenge. If you have a person or two in your life who are mature in faith and really care about you, consider meeting with them and humbly inviting them to speak truth into your life ... any time. Let them know that you will seek to prayerfully listen and receive their words, even when those words are difficult.

Read for Next Session

Take time before your next small group to read chapter 13 of *The Story*.

SESSION 13

The King Who Had It All

Starting well is easy.
Finishing well is a lifelong project
that many do not complete.

Introduction

Do you remember the childhood make-believe game called "Three Wishes"? This game involved making any three wishes, big or small. "I wish for a new bike." "I wish I could walk through walls or fly like Superman!" "I wish I could see my dad, who has been gone for so long."

When we were young, just three wishes could satisfy our childlike imagination. As time passed and we grew up, we got smarter. Some of us figured out that we only really needed one wish answered. Do you remember what that one wish was? "I want an endless supply of wishes," of course!

A rare few kids, with time, would devote one of their wishes to solving world hunger or bringing world peace. But honestly, most of us just asked for an infinite supply of wishes so we could make sure we got whatever we wanted for the rest of our lives.

In chapter 13 of *The Story* God appears to the third king of Israel, David's son Solomon. God actually tells him, "You can ask for anything from me and I will give it to you." What Solomon requests is an amazing example to all of us.

Talk About It

If you were playing the wish game and could be given one super power that would enable you to help others, what would it be?

DVD Teaching Notes

As you watch the video segment for session 13, use the following outline to record anything that stands out to you.

King Solomon wisely asks for wisdom

Solomon builds the temple

Solomon's proverbial pot of lukewarm water

Solomon's conclusion in the book of Ecclesiastes

DVD Discussion

1. Our culture can be a little like the kettle and we can become the frogs plopped into the water ... if we are not careful. Name some examples of dangerous and incremental changes happening around us that we can fail to notice. What can we do to wake up, notice, and resist these changes?

> *If Solomon was the wisest guy to ever live and he did not notice when he became a frog in a kettle, what makes us think we are too smart to do such a thing?*

2. As David neared the end of his life, he gave a charge to his son Solomon (1 Kings 2:1 – 4; *The Story*, p. 176). What were his specific exhortations and how do these words reflect what David had learned from his personal choices in life?

3. God appeared to Solomon in a dream and engaged him in the "If you could have anything you want" conversation (1 Kings 3:5 – 14; *The Story*, pp. 176 – 177). What did Solomon ask for and what did he refrain from asking for? What can we learn about prayer from this account in Solomon's life?

4. As Solomon's wisdom grew, the Holy Spirit inspired him to write and collect wise sayings. According to Proverbs 1:1 – 7 (*The Story*, p. 179), what is the purpose and value of the proverbs and why are they needed just as much today as they were in ancient times?

5. *The Story* (pp. 179 – 183) includes many examples of proverbs. Respond to *one* of the questions below about this collection of wise sayings:
   - What do they teach us about *fearing God*?
   - What do they teach us about *God-honoring relationships*?
   - What do they teach us about *how to handle our finances wisely*?
   - What do they teach us about *how we use our words*?

6. As the temple was dedicated, Solomon prayed and spoke to the people of Israel (1 Kings 8:22 – 61; *The Story*, pp. 186 – 188). What do his words teach us about God? What does he ask for himself and for the people, and how can his prayer inform the way we speak with God?

7. After Solomon's prayer and charge to the people, God spoke (1 Kings 9:1 – 9; *The Story*, pp. 188 – 189). What promises did God give the people

("If you do this … I will do this")? How did these promises give both hope and a sober awareness of their need to follow God closely?

8. At the end of his life, the wise King Solomon did some very foolish things (1 Kings 11:1 – 13; *The Story*, pp. 191 – 192). What did he do and what were some of the consequences? How can we avoid finishing poorly?

   Is there some area of your life you would like your small group to pray for you to continue living wisely or to redirect you so you can live and finish strong?

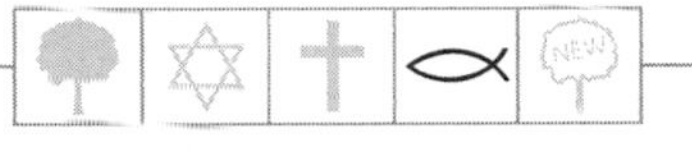

9. Read movement 4 of *The Story* (p. 11 of this participant's guide). How does God unfold his story in this fourth movement and how does this connect with your story?

How we live our lives matters. Our prayer needs to be that we will not only start strong but finish strong.

Closing Prayer

As you take time to pray, here are some ideas to get you started:

- Ask God to help you grow in his wisdom more and more with each passing day.
- Invite the Holy Spirit to open your eyes to any kettles of slow-boiling water that you might be in right now. Pray for strength to hop out today!
- Thank God for the wise people he has placed in your life and ask him to help you become someone who can offer wisdom to the next generation.

Between Sessions

Personal Reflections

Near the end of his life, Solomon was inspired by God to write a collection of reflections, the book of Ecclesiastes, on what he learned along the way. Read Ecclesiastes and reflect on how easy it is to focus on the wrong stuff. Ask God to help you identify what matters most to him and what should be most important to you.

Personal Action

Give a charge (some words of wisdom) to a young person in your life. Prayerfully identify one or two people that God might want to encourage through your words, meet with them, and share what God places on your heart.

The book of Proverbs is thirty-one chapters long. Consider making a commitment to read one chapter of it each day for the coming month. It will take just a few minutes per day. As you read this amazing book you will grow in wisdom.

Read for Next Session

Take time before your next small group to read chapter 14 of *The Story.*

SESSION 14

A Kingdom Torn in Two

There is nothing civil about a civil war.

Introduction

In the Gettysburg Address, November 19, 1863, Abraham Lincoln said:

> Four score and seven years ago our fathers brought forth on this continent a new nation, conceived in liberty, and dedicated to the proposition that all men are created equal. Now we are engaged in a great civil war, testing whether that nation, or any nation, so conceived and so dedicated, can long endure. We are met on a great battlefield of that war. We have come to dedicate a portion of that field, as a final resting-place for those who here gave their lives that that nation might live. It is altogether fitting and proper that we should do this.

The American Civil War pitted brother against brother, sister against sister. In a civil war, everyone who dies is from the same nation ... in a sense, from the same family.

Chapter 14 of *The Story* captures the painful and heart-wrenching account of a divided nation ... God's people Israel. The American Civil War spanned four years; Israel's lasted over two hundred. In America, the war ended with a unified nation (over time). In Israel, the two factions never united again.

God desires unity in nations, workplaces, schools, neighborhoods, churches, and homes. He invites us to be instruments of peace and to seek harmony in our relationships. Accomplishing this involves a lifelong commitment to follow God and seek his help. We can't do this on our own.

Talk About It

Chapter 14 of *The Story* unfolds like an epic Hollywood drama: conflict, intrigue, war, and flashes of redemption amidst heartbreaking rebellion. Tell about a movie you enjoyed that has strong redemptive themes. What is one life lesson that can be learned from this movie?

DVD Teaching Notes

As you watch the video segment for session 14, use the following outline to record anything that stands out to you.

Setting for the story

Main characters: meeting Rehoboam and Jeroboam

Lower Story plot, resolution, and theme

Upper Story plot, resolution, and theme

DVD Discussion

1. When Solomon's son, Rehoboam, was faced with a decision about the heavy taxes he was placing on the people, he sought two sources of input (1 Kings 12:1 – 11; *The Story*, pp. 193 – 194). What was each source and how did their advice conflict? Why do you think the advice was so radically different?

2. Older people who have walked longer in life often carry a body of wisdom in their heart. Who is a very wise person you know and how has he or she impacted your life? What is one of the best pieces of wisdom this person has offered you through the years?

3. In their wisdom, the elders told Rehoboam that if he served the nation, the people would gladly follow him. Jesus modeled this truth in the New Testament when he washed the disciples' feet (John 13). How can serving with a humble heart actually make a person a stronger leader?

   What are ways you could grow in service as you seek to influence the lives of the people around you? Who is one person God is calling you to serve this week?

4. This section of *The Story* as well as the teaching and life of Jesus illustrate that a divided house will always fall. What practical things can we do to bring peace in our family and within our homes?

Satan loves to divide families. If the enemy has created conflict in your family (or is trying to do so), how can you battle against this and seek healing and peace?

5. The church, the family of God, has had its own share of civil wars and divisions through the centuries. What can you do to seek peace and harmony in your local church?

A house divided against itself can't stand. We need to do our part in making sure this is not happening in our home, our church, or our nation.

6. From the perspective of the Lower Story, the division in the kingdom was a result of Rehoboam's harsh leadership style. From the Upper Story, we know that Solomon's idolatry and compromise were cascading like a line of dominos into the nation's future. What can we learn from the wrong attitudes and actions of both father and son in this story?

7. Randy noted, "Whenever Israel was fully devoted to God, they were strong and prospered; but when they divided their loyalty with other gods or interests, they were weakened." How do you see this spiritual reality alive in chapter 14 of *The Story* and in your own life?

> *To experience the full blessings of God, to ensure that everything works out for the good in our life, we need to love God above all and align our lives to his Upper Story plan.*

8. As this chapter of *The Story* shows, the sin of spiritual compromise through idolatry is of great concern to God. It led to Solomon's poor finish in life. It also marked both the Northern Kingdom of Israel and the Southern Kingdom of Judah and eventually led to the fall of both. What are ways that idolatry can still slip into our lives today? How can we identify it and root it out before it weakens our faith and destroys us?

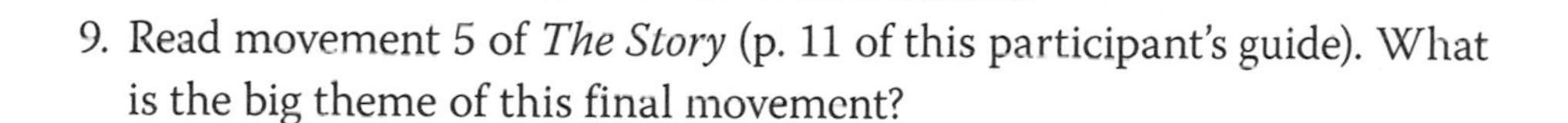

9. Read movement 5 of *The Story* (p. 11 of this participant's guide). What is the big theme of this final movement?

Closing Prayer

As you take time to pray, here are some ideas to get you started:

- Thank God that despite human failures throughout history, he has never given up on us but continues seeking and loving us.
- Thank God for the people he has placed in your life who have real wisdom and are willing to share it with you.
- Pray for healing in your relationships that are broken.

Between Sessions

Personal Reflections

Meditate this week on these three questions:

- Am I a peacemaker or a source of conflict in my relationships and how can I seek to build bridges and heal broken relationships in my life?
- When I am placed in situations where I am called to be an influencer and leader, am I a humble servant?
- Are there any idols in my life ... even little ones? If so, what can I do to cast them out?

Personal Action

One of the most divisive organizations in the history of the world, sadly, has been the church. As you move about your community in the coming week, commit to pray for every church you pass. Ask for God's blessing and guidance for these brothers and sisters.

Read for Next Session

Take time before your next small group to read chapter 15 of *The Story.*

God's Messengers

The late Supreme Court justice Oliver Wendell Holmes, Jr.
is often misquoted as saying it is wrong to shout "fire"
in a crowded movie house. What he actually said was that
it is wrong to falsely shout "fire" in a crowded movie house.

Introduction

A well-placed, clearly written sign can keep you safe and even save your life. Just think about it: we all appreciate signs that are intended to protect us when danger is near. Here are some examples:

- Beware of Dog
- Slippery When Wet
- Thin Ice
- This Product May Cause Cancer
- Bridge Out

In chapter 15 of *The Story* we meet God's signposts — the prophets. God lovingly placed them right in the middle of the roads where his people walked so their voices could give clear warnings. These men were faithful, passionate, and relentless. Sometimes the people listened. Often they went right past the signpost, ignored the prophets, and drove off a cliff.

Over and over God would send his messengers, the prophets. God's plan never changed. He wanted to bring the people back into loving relationship with him. As the prophets spoke, the cry of God's heart could be heard: "Please come home; turn from your sin; return to me; I still love you; it is not too late."

Talk About It

Tell about a time you saw a sign, followed what it said, and were glad you did. Or, tell about a time you missed or ignored a posted sign and suffered for it.

DVD Teaching Notes

As you watch the video segment for session 15, use the following outline to record anything that stands out to you.

The reason God divided the nation of Israel

The Northern Kingdom (Israel) and the Southern Kingdom (Judah)

The prophets enter to give a loving and clear message from God

Hosea's voice … God speaks; Hosea's life … God's message

DVD Discussion

1. God still loves his people, still tenderly seeks to warn us when we are in danger. Name some ways God posts a warning sign in the middle of the road as we travel through life.

2. When Elijah challenged the false prophets of Baal, at one point he turned to all the people of Israel and asked, "How long will you waver between two opinions? If the LORD is God, follow him; but if Baal is God, follow him" (1 Kings 18:21; *The Story*, p. 204). What can it look like in our day when Christians "waver between two opinions," trying to keep one foot in the world while still trying to walk with Jesus? How does such a lifestyle keep us from really experiencing intimate friendship with God?

3. Right after an amazing victory, Elijah faced one of his hardest times both spiritually and emotionally (1 Kings 19:1 – 9; *The Story*, pp. 206 – 207). What did Elijah go through (emotionally, physically, and spiritually) and how did God seek to lovingly restore him?

   Tell about a time you hit a low spot in your faith shortly after a time of real victory or strength. How can we be on our guard and prepared for spiritual attack in instances like these?

4. Describe the Upper Story and the Lower Story as you follow Elisha and his servant through the account told in 2 Kings 6:8 – 23 (*The Story*, pp. 211 – 212). Why is it important for us to pray for spiritual eyes that can occasionally get a glimpse of what is happening in the Upper Story?

5. Through the prophets Amos and Hosea, God pointed out the people's sin and actions of rebellion (*The Story*, pp. 213 – 217). What were some of Israel's sins and why do you think God was being so severe with them?

God still speaks today. He's calling. The question is whether or not you will pick up his call and listen or send God into voicemail.

6. It is clear that if God's people will repent (turn from sin and return to him) God is ready to embrace them with love and grace. How is God still offering this same invitation through Jesus today? What does true repentance and turning back to God look like, in light of the cross of Jesus?

7. When Israel walked closely with God, they were joy-filled and fruitful. When they were distracted by other pursuits (including false gods and idols), their whole community life went sour. How does your life, including your attitude and general disposition, change when you are not walking closely with Jesus?

> *The secret of Israel's success was their God. Their relationship with him was meant to cause other nations to say, "We want to get to know this God too!"*

8. How does reading and following the teaching of the Bible keep us connected to God and guard our hearts against the kind of complacency Israel experienced? What can we do to deepen our commitment to study and obey God's Word?

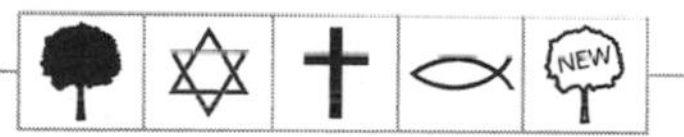

9. Read movements 1–5 of *The Story* (pp. 10–11 of this participant's guide). How do these five movements form a full and beautiful story?

Closing Prayer

As you take time to pray, here are some ideas to get you started:

- Ask God to open your eyes (like he did for Elisha's servant) so that you can see what is happening in the Upper Story. This can be very encouraging!
- Thank God for his loving discipline and relentless pursuit of a healthy relationship with you.
- Ask for a soft heart that is ready to repent and turn back to God as soon as you see areas of rebellion and sin in your life.

Between Sessions

Personal Reflections

God was very patient with the nation Israel. For over two centuries and through the reigns of nineteen kings, God kept loving, seeking, and sending his prophets with a call for his people to come home. Finally, God said, "Enough!" and accomplished his plan of restored relationship with humanity through the Southern Kingdom of Judah. Reflect on how patient God has been with you. Identify patterns of sin in your life that seem to come back again and again. Pray for power to see these and turn from them.

Personal Action

God is calling. Don't put him into voicemail. This week sit quietly in prayer and listen to God, a journal or blank piece of paper and pen in hand. Ask God a few simple, pointed questions and write down any words he places on your heart. Here are a few questions to get you started:

- What have you done to show your love and patience with me? (Thank him.)
- What are the behaviors and attitudes in my life that are not honoring to you? (Commit to change.)
- How can I listen more closely to your Word (the Bible) and other ways you speak to me? (Seek to follow his leading ... even when it is hard.)

Read for Next Session

Take time before your next small group to read chapter 16 of *The Story.*

SESSION 16

The Beginning of the End
(of the Kingdom of Israel)

Even when things seem hopeless,
prayer still makes a difference. Give it a try!

Introduction

With ten minutes left in a basketball game and one team down by thirty points, people begin leaving the gym because they can see the handwriting on the wall. If a football team is behind by three touchdowns at the two-minute warning, even committed fans will slide out of their seats and head to the parking lot to try to beat the traffic.

When a game is close and the outcome is still up for grabs, people stay glued to their seats. No one knows how it will end. But when one team is running away with a landslide victory, people lose interest very quickly.

What is true in the world of sports also is evident in the pages of *The Story*. At a certain point, the Northern Kingdom of Israel was in such bad shape, so rebellious, that there was no way they were going to turn around. Using a sports analogy, there was still time on the clock, but the end results were clear for everyone to see. Even the Southern Kingdom of Judah hit a point where things looked hopeless. But sometimes a team can rally ... even when it looks like there is no chance of a comeback!

Talk About It

Tell about a time you watched a sporting event that looked like it was over, but a team that seemed defeated made an amazing comeback.

DVD Teaching Notes

As you watch the video segment for session 16, use the following outline to record anything that stands out to you.

"No king but King Jesus"

The beginning of the end for Israel, the Northern Kingdom

King Hezekiah: one of the Southern Kingdom's good kings

Isaiah's proclamation of God's purpose

DVD Discussion

1. Chapter 16 of *The Story* covers more than two hundred years. The Northern Kingdom of Israel fell to the Assyrians in 722 BC and was never heard from again. The Southern Kingdom of Judah fell to the Babylonians in 586 BC but had an amazing comeback seventy years later when they returned from captivity. How do you see God's patience and commitment to bring his people back to himself woven through these two centuries of history?

> *We see over and over again in the Bible, Old and New Testaments, that when we put God on the throne of our lives, we put ourselves in the best possible position for success.*

2. God allowed a foreign army to invade and defeat Israel (the Northern Kingdom). Why did God bring this judgment on his own people and what do you learn from God's response to the behavior of Israel (2 Kings 17:1–14; *The Story*, pp. 219–220)?

3. Hezekiah of Judah was one of the few kings deemed "good" in the eyes of God (2 Kings 18–19; *The Story*, pp. 220–224). What did Hezekiah do that pleased God and how can we learn from his example? How can Hezekiah's prayer shape the way you pray when times are tough?

4. The Bible has a lot to say about pride. What do you learn about pride in the encounter between Assyria and Israel in this chapter of *The Story*?

   What is one way we can avoid pride and grow in humility?

5. Though the Southern Kingdom of Judah discovered they would one day end up prisoners of war under the fist of a foreign nation, God spoke words of hope through his prophet (Isaiah 14:1 – 5; Isaiah 49; *The Story*, pp. 226 – 228). What did God promise and how do you see him continuing to accomplish his plan to bring his people back to himself?

6. The final and greatest hope for all of God's people, including you and me, is the promise of the Messiah who would come to deliver us (Isaiah 53; *The Story*, pp. 228 – 230). What do you learn about Jesus, the promised Savior, from this prophecy?

   How has Jesus been the One who brings your life hope and meaning?

"No king but King Jesus!"

7. Hezekiah pleased God when he spiritually cleaned house, got rid of idols, and smashed and cut down all the signs of spiritual compromise in the land. When you look at your spiritual life, what could you clean out, cut down, or smash so that you can walk more closely with God?

8. When Jerusalem was surrounded by the Assyrian army and the situation looked hopeless, Hezekiah prayed and things changed. What are you facing today that seems too big, overwhelming, or even hopeless, and how can your group members join you in prayer?

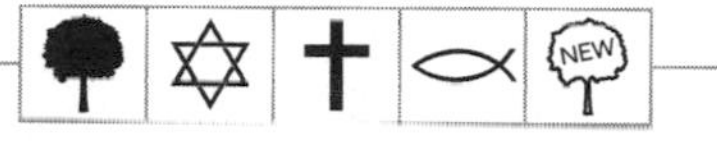

9. Read movements 1 – 5 of *The Story* (pp. 10 – 11 of this participant's guide). How does your personal journey of faith parallel the movements of *The Story*?

Closing Prayer

As you take time to pray, here are some ideas to get you started:

- Praise Jesus for being the Messiah, the One who brings hope to a hopeless world.
- Ask God to take you to deeper places as a person of prayer. Invite the Holy Spirit to teach you to pray with greater passion.
- Lift up members of your group who are facing difficult situations and pray for God's presence, power, and plan to be unleashed in their lives.

Between Sessions

Personal Reflections

Over and over the people of Israel let idolatry creep into their lives, homes, culture — even their worship. They seemed blind to what they were doing. This week reflect on your lifestyle, choices, hobbies, loves. Is anything becoming an idol, dominating your passion and time to the point that you're not growing in your relationship with Jesus? If so, read 2 Kings 23:1 – 30, the account of another good king of Judah who did some serious housecleaning to rid idolatry from the land. Compare his passion, zeal, and thoroughness as you consider how you can ensure your life is free of idolatry.

Personal Action

Every morning when you wake up, for the next week, make this simple statement before you get out of bed: "No king but King Jesus!" Then seek to live out this truth each day.

Read for Next Session

Take time before your next small group to read chapter 17 of *The Story.*

SESSION 17

The Kingdoms' Fall

Jeremiah had good reason to weep,
but God has the remedy to wipe tears away!

Introduction

Have you ever watched a movie and found yourself thinking, somewhere near the conclusion, "There has to be a catch. This can't be the way the story ends"?

This is what happens in the classic movie *E.T.* Near the end, the star of the show, the cute little extraterrestrial character, dies. His glowing heart stops glowing; his radiant pointer finger goes dark; his alien skin turns pasty. Our Reese's Pieces-eating gentle hero just dies.

Everyone knows this is wrong. You can feel it in the air. The story can't end like this. There must be some surprise, some hope, some twist or turn coming ... there *must* be!

Chapter 17 of *The Story* is just such a moment. The Northern Kingdom of Israel will disappear forever. The Southern Kingdom of Judah will be invaded by Babylon and taken captive. The city of Jerusalem and Solomon's temple will be destroyed.

We read along and say, "This can't be the end! God promised to bring people back to himself and accomplish his plan ... through Israel. Isn't there some surprise twist or turn? Is there still hope for God's plan?"

The answer to these questions will be examined in chapter 19 of *The Story* (but don't rush ahead to find out!).

Talk About It

Tell about a movie you saw or book you read in which you neared the end and things seemed to be concluding all wrong. How did things actually turn out?

DVD Teaching Notes

As you watch the video segment for session 17, use the following outline to record anything that stands out to you.

How Israel got to their "no remedy" moment

Jeremiah's assignment in God's Upper Story

Ezekiel and Jeremiah speak

The bright spot in a dark time of history ... there is still hope!

DVD Discussion

1. In the DVD segment Randy said, "For hundreds of years God waited patiently, warned his people, and gave them chance after chance." Why was God so patient with the people of Israel when they were so rebellious and sinful? How have you experienced God's great patience in your life?

2. In the prophet Ezekiel's amazing and powerful vision from God (Ezekiel 1, 2, 6; *The Story,* pp. 235–237), what do we learn about the following:
   - The condition of the people's hearts (the nation of Judah)
   - The reasons for the coming judgment
   - What lies ahead for Judah and Jerusalem

3. How can God's discipline of his children be the best gift he can give us? How has God disciplined you on your journey of faith and how did his loving discipline help you grow?

With God's people there is never a strong, truthful bout of loving discipline without God's grace following right behind it. It was true for Judah. It is true for us.

4. Once Jerusalem had fallen and the Babylonians had utterly destroyed the nation of Judah, Jeremiah recorded what he saw and felt (Lamentations 1–5; *The Story*, pp. 243–245). What did he write that made the situation seem hopeless, like it was all over? What did he write that seemed to have a sense of hope, like God's plan could still be accomplished?

5. When God called Jeremiah to serve him, he assured him that his plan had been in place since Jeremiah was in his mother's womb. In the New Testament we learn that God has a plan for each of us who follow him. How has God gifted and called you to serve him and how are you following this call? How can your group members pray for you and cheer you on as you seek to follow God with greater faithfulness and passion?

> *"For we are God's handiwork, created in Christ Jesus to do good works, which God prepared in advance for us to do." (Ephesians 2:10)*

6. As with many of the people God calls (in the Bible and in the world today), Jeremiah had his list of excuses. What excuses do we use to try to get out of following God? How can we encourage each other to stop making excuses and boldly follow God's leading?

7. In one of the most hopeless times in biblical history, the prophet Ezekiel pointed ahead to a future time when the story's ending will be rewritten (Ezekiel 36:1 – 37:14; *The Story,* pp. 245 – 247). How do Ezekiel's words bring hope when it feels as if the story is over?

8. Respond to this statement: "In God's employment contract he does not ask us to be successful (by the world's standards) but faithful. Success is based on faithfulness to God . . . not the results!" What is one way you can be more faithful to God in the coming weeks? How can your group members encourage you in this effort?

9. Read movement 3 of *The Story* (p. 11 of this participant's guide). If one of your group members has memorized this short statement that describes the heartbeat of the third movement, allow them to quote it and tell about what God taught them as they committed this statement to memory.

Closing Prayer

As you take time to pray, here are some ideas to get you started:

- Thank God that he is the One who can bring hope, even in the times when it feels like there is no remedy.
- Ask God to speak to your heart as you read the words of the prophets. If there are areas of resistance or rebellion, invite the conviction of God's Word to cut through them and open your heart to repentance.
- Ezekiel expresses God's desire for the nations to know that he is the Sovereign Lord. Ask God to use your life as a signpost to declare his might, presence, love, and sovereignty.

Between Sessions

Personal Reflections

Jeremiah knew that God had a plan for him, even when he was in his mother's womb. The apostle Paul assured all believers that God has prepared good works for each of us to do. In the coming week ask God to help you see his plans for your life. If there is an action, commitment, or adventure that you have been resisting, surrender and follow him!

Personal Action

Hezekiah had children who were not faithful and so did Josiah. We see this pattern throughout *The Story* with some very godly leaders, including Eli and Samuel. Identify teens or adults in your own family who have wandered from God. Pray for them. As applicable, consider giving them a call, sending a note of encouragement, or spending time with them. Ask God to use you to extend his message of grace.

Read for Next Session

Take time before your next small group to read chapter 18 of *The Story*.

SESSION 18

Daniel in Exile

Integrity is who you are
when no one is looking!

Introduction

The Story features a surprising array of people who have amazing integrity, and others who seem to have none at all. Remember the young man Joseph (chapter 3) who was sold as a slave (by his own brothers) and became a prisoner in a foreign land. Far from home, with no family members or friends around to encourage or critique him, Joseph led a life of staggering integrity. He resisted temptation even though no one would have known ... except God.

Here in chapter 18 we encounter four young men from Judah who have been exiled in the capital city of their sworn enemies. They were in a place where "no one was looking." They could compromise and cut corners and no one would ever know ... except God.

Integrity can seem like an antiquated value in our modern world. Every day we have opportunities to make little concessions. Indeed, our culture invites and encourages compromise:

"You won't get caught."

"It's no big deal ... everyone is doing it."

"It's the price of doing business."

"Lighten up; no one else cares about that, why should you?"

"No one will ever know!"

Then we hear the same still small voice that spoke to Joseph in prison and Daniel and his three friends in captivity. "I see. I care. I love you. Stand strong."

Talk About It

All sorts of voices in our culture cry out, inviting us to compromise our faith. What are some of these messages?

DVD Teaching Notes

As you watch the video segment for session 18, use the following outline to record anything that stands out to you.

In the Lower Story Daniel finds himself away from home

King Nebuchadnezzar's demand creates a fiery ordeal

Daniel and the lion's den

In the Upper Story we find ourselves away from home

DVD Discussion

1. When Daniel and his three friends became prisoners of war, they were pressured to change many things as part of their "training" process (Daniel 1; *The Story*, pp. 249 – 250). What concessions were they willing to make and where did they draw the line and say no? Why do you think they drew the line where they did?

   What is an example of an area where you have said, "I draw the line here and I will not cross it"? What has happened as you have made this stand and maintained your integrity?

> *"Dear friends, I urge you, as foreigners and exiles, to abstain from sinful desires, which wage war against your soul. Live such good lives among the pagans that, though they accuse you of doing wrong, they may see your good deeds and glorify God on the day he visits us." (1 Peter 2:11 – 12)*

2. When Daniel heard of King Nebuchadnezzar's seemingly impossible request (Daniel 2:1 – 18; *The Story*, pp. 250 – 252), he asked his three friends to pray and seek the face of God with him. Why is prayer the right response in this critical moment of Daniel's story? What is one situation you are facing right now that needs prayer and how can your group members support you in this way?

3. Once God answered the prayers of Daniel and his friends, Daniel lifted up an amazing prayer of praise (Daniel 2:20 – 23; *The Story*, p. 252). What do you learn about Daniel's understanding of God in this prayer and how might this shape the way you pray?

4. As Daniel explained the king's dream and its interpretation, he was careful to not take credit but give all the glory to God (Daniel 2:27 – 30; *The Story*, pp. 252 – 253). In what ways can we be tempted to take credit for what God does? How can we give him the glory instead?

5. Shadrach, Meshach, and Abednego stood face-to-face with King Nebuchadnezzar and told him they would not bow down and commit idolatry, even if it cost them their lives. Where does this kind of strength and integrity come from? Tell about a situation where you faced (or are facing) real pressure to compromise biblical truth.

6. When Shadrach, Meshach, and Abednego ended up in the furnace, they discovered they were not alone (Daniel 3:25; *The Story*, pp. 256). Describe a furnace time in your life when God showed up in a very personal and powerful way.

7. Despite Daniel's Lower Story struggle of persecution and oppression, what were some of the ways God was working in the Upper Story? Why is it so important that we slow down occasionally and take note of how God is working in the Upper Story of our lives?

> *In the Lower Story the king throws Daniel in the lion's den for not bowing to him; in the Upper Story the King of Kings closes the mouth of the lions for bowing only to him.*

8. It is in the dark places that light shines most brightly. What are some ways we can be part of our culture and still not compromise? Why is it valuable and even essential for Christians to understand and function within our culture (without crossing the line of compromise) if we are going to bring Jesus' message and love to this world? Where is one place in your life that God wants his light to shine through you?

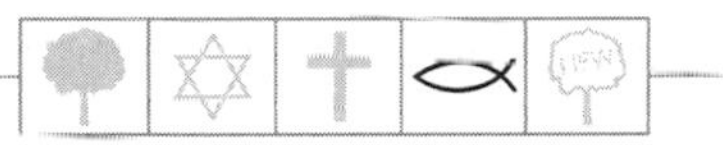

9. Read movement 4 of *The Story* (p. 11 of this participant's guide). How has your connection in the local church brought you closer to Jesus and more aware of his plan to reach all people with his love?

Closing Prayer

As you take time to pray, here are some ideas to get you started:

- Lift up the needs and situations expressed by your group members in discussion question 2.
- Pray for power to stand strong in your faith even when culture and people around you pressure you to compromise.
- Thank God that he is with you even in the furnace moments of life.

Between Sessions

Personal Reflections

Shadrach, Meshach, and Abednego boldly declared that they would die before bowing down to an idol. Think about some of the pressure-filled situations in your life and the ways you are tempted to compromise. Ask God to give you a passionate commitment to holiness and a life of integrity. Prepare yourself to stand strong ... no matter what you face.

Personal Action

Daniel, Shadrach, Meshach, and Abednego had each other. Though prisoners of war, this small community of faithful friends could band together in prayer and obedience. Make work of building this kind of network in your life. If you have one, be intentional about strengthening it. If you don't, begin praying for and looking for people of integrity who can become long-term friends and supporters.

Read for Next Session

Take time before your next small group to read chapter 19 of *The Story.*

SESSION 19

The Return Home

Sometimes, when hope seems dead
and the darkness of night closes in strong against us,
God is about to do something really big.

Introduction

Remember the introduction from session 17 — about how some movies feel like they are about to end wrong? Near the conclusion of the classic *E.T.*, the heroic little alien dies. His finger will not glow; his body lies pale and lifeless.

In shock, the audience waits for something to happen. Things can't end like this. "Wake up, E.T.! Get up!" Finally, as the music builds to a crescendo, hope returns. E.T. is alive! He has phoned home. His friends are coming. He glows again. The movie's suspense, though only minutes, seemed to last forever.

In *The Story*, the people of Israel awaited their "resurrection" from exile not seconds, minutes, hours, or days. Hope did not return in weeks, a few months, or even a decade. The people of God waited for seventy years ... almost two generations!

Finally, God's plan to bring his people back to himself began again. God raised up prophets and leaders who loved him and glowed with his holy presence. Boldness was breathed into the people and hope returned. This was the long-awaited moment when the people of Israel would return to the Promised Land, rebuild the city of Jerusalem, and experience the grace of God in ways they had longed for over their decades of exile.

Talk About It

Tell about an experience when you waited a long time for God to take action or answer a prayer. How did you meet God in the waiting and in the time when he finally answered?

DVD Teaching Notes

As you watch the video segment for session 19, use the following outline to record anything that stands out to you.

Returning home

The temple as a divine teaching aid

Sidetracked

Giving careful thoughts to your ways

DVD Discussion

1. In the DVD segment Randy pointed out that God was "pulling some strings in the Upper Story" (putting King Cyrus on the throne) so that he could make changes in the Lower Story (set the exiles free). Give an example of a time in your life when you know that God was moving in the Upper Story so that he could accomplish something in your Lower Story.

2. Randy talked about how God's big thing can become our little thing if we are not careful. When this happens, we get off track. What are examples of how God's big thing can become our little thing? What can we do to make sure we are really seeking to keep God's big thing on the front burner of our heart and life?

> *Give careful thoughts to your ways.*
> *Evaluate your priorities.*
> *Assess your strategies.*
> *"Is God's big thing my big thing?"*

3. When the people of Israel began working on the foundation of the temple (Ezra 4; *The Story*, p. 265) they met resistance. What kind of conflict and opposition did the people face? When we seek to follow God's will with a passionate heart, what resistance might we face?

4. Eventually the people got sidetracked from rebuilding God's temple. It was sixteen years before he finally got them back on track (Haggai 1; *The Story*, pp. 266–267). What slowed down their work and what got them up and moving again?

   What are some of the consequences we face when we do our own thing and forget to follow God's plan for our lives?

> *When nothing quenches our deepest thirsts,*
> *when no achievements abate our restless hunger,*
> *when droughts turn our fields into deserts and retirements*
> *into pocket change, what can we do? God's answer is clear.*
> *"Give careful thoughts to your ways."*

5. What did God promise the people if they would move forward with his work (Haggai 2; *The Story*, pp. 267–268)? How does this bring you hope and inspiration to walk in obedience to God's leading?

6. The end of this chapter of *The Story* offers a glimpse of the political wrangling that took place behind the scenes. The governor of the region wanted the people to stop building the temple and accused them of

having no permission to build it. After communication with the king of Babylon, everything changed—and, remember, there were no phones or email (Ezra 5–6; *The Story*, pp. 270–273). How did God turn everything upside down and provide for the temple? How do you see the Upper Story breaking into the Lower Story again?

7. God called the people to action through his prophets such as Haggai, who told them to get up to the hills, gather wood, and begin building … pretty practical stuff! What is one next step you need to take to "gather wood" and start building into God's plan for your life? How can your group members pray for you and encourage you as you take this step?

8. Read movement 5 of *The Story* (p. 11 of this participant's guide). How does God unfold his story in this fifth movement and how does this connect with your story?

Closing Prayer

As you take time to pray, here are some ideas to get you started:

- Confess where you have made God's big thing a secondhand concern.
- Pray for strength to do what it takes to follow God's will for your life.
- Ask God to dwell right in the middle of your life and be so present that the world will see him alive in you.

Between Sessions

Personal Reflections

Haggai called the people to "give careful thought to [their] ways" and wake up to the reality that God was not blessing them because they were not following him. In the coming week give careful thought to your ways. Reflect on the following questions:

- Is God's big thing my big thing?
- Am I building my house or God's house?
- Are my priorities in order?
- What can I do to make sure God is first in my heart, schedule, and actions?

Personal Action

Haggai called the people to go up to the hills and gather timber (the supplies they needed to build the temple). Spend a few minutes listing some things you need to "gather" so that you can serve God with all your heart. It might be a new attitude, an altered schedule, a tender heart, or a generous lifestyle. Then commit to "gather" these things so that you can build a new future with God right in the center!

Read for Next Session

Take time before your next small group to read chapter 20 of *The Story*.

SESSION 20

The Queen of Beauty and Courage

God is near, present, and working …
even when we can't see him.

Introduction

You might remember the *Where's Waldo?* phenomenon a number of years ago. Each spread of every *Where's Waldo?* picture book was filled with people going about their business … at the zoo, in the museum, on the beach. But somewhere among them was Waldo. If you looked closely and studied the picture long enough, you would finally find his red-and-white striped shirt, blue pants, brown shoes, bobble hat, unique haircut, and distinctive eyeglasses.

With time, looking for this silly character became an international craze. The Icelandic people looked for Valli, the Norwegians scoured the pages for Willy, the French searched for Charlie, and Israelis played *Where's Efi?* The fun of these books was the process of looking for, and finally finding, Waldo.

Similarly, as we read each chapter of *The Story,* we discover that God is on every page, at work each moment, and present at all times … even when he is hard to see. Chapter 20 is the account of Esther. This Bible book is unique because, in the full text of Esther's story, the name of God is never used … not once.

Esther and her people faced a horrific threat in a foreign land. The story is an intrigue of persecution, conflict, a vicious enemy, twists and turns, and vindication. Yet despite the seeming absence of God, he is everywhere in Esther's story. The same is true in our story today… even when we don't notice him.

Talk About It

Books such as *Where's Waldo?* and games such as hide-and-seek are great fun. But tell about a time you actually lost a real person (or got lost) and what it took to find them (or find your way again).

DVD Teaching Notes

As you watch the video segment for session 20, use the following outline to record anything that stands out to you.

The background of Esther's story and why Haman hated the Jews

Plotting against the Jews and an irreversible edict of doom

When the Lower Story seems hopeless, God is still writing an Upper Story

Esther comes on the scene "for such a time as this"

DVD Discussion

1. What were some of the cultural norms and laws that came into play in this chapter of *The Story* (for Vashti, for Haman, for the Jews), and why is it important for believers today to understand our culture as we seek to be God's presence and messengers of his grace?

2. What drives a person like Haman and how have you had to negotiate a relationship with a person with similar motivations? What wisdom would you give a Christian who is forced to work, live, and exist around a Haman-like personality?

Haman rolled the dice, but God determined how the dice would fall.

3. What characteristics marked the life and behavior of Mordecai? How can we take steps to grow character like Mordecai as we seek to follow God's Upper Story in our Lower Story lives?

4. Throughout this entire chapter, what strikes you about Esther's character, how she related to people, and the risks she took? What can we learn and gain from her example?

5. Eventually a great and radical reversal happened between Haman and Mordecai (Esther 5 – 7; *The Story*, pp. 282 – 285). How do you see God's hand at work bringing his Upper Story plan into the Lower Story of Haman's plots and schemes?

   Tell about a time when you faced a situation that seemed hopeless (from a Lower Story, human perspective), but God miraculously turned things around. What helped you see God's presence and power at work as you walked through this situation?

6. In one of *The Story*'s epic moments, Esther resolved in her heart to approach the king, reveal her national identity, and make an appeal for her people — despite the great risk involved. She concluded, "If I perish, I perish." Christians are called to "take up their cross daily" and follow Jesus (Luke 9:23). What is a risk God is calling you to take for him and how can group members stand with you as you follow God's leading?

7. A lesson from Esther's story is that God is going to accomplish his will, with or without us (Esther 4:12 – 14; *The Story*, p. 282). Tell about a time you entered into God's story and got to be part of his plan *or* tell about a time you opted out and missed an opportunity to be part of God's story.

God wants us to stand up with courage for what is right, like Esther did—we need to know that we too were called "for such a time as this" to fulfill God's plan.

8. At the end of this chapter, we read that God did not remove the danger of attack on the Jews, but provided a chance for them to fight back and defend themselves. What is a battle (against culture, world systems, or some evil) that God is calling you to fight? How can your group members pray for you and enter the battle with you?

9. Read movements 1 – 5 of *The Story* (pp. 10 – 11 of this participant's guide). How is God moving in the Lower Story in each movement?

Closing Prayer

As you take time to pray, here are some ideas to get you started:

- Thank God that he is present on every page of your life, even if you don't actually see him.
- Ask for wisdom to see when God has placed you in a specific place at a specific time to do a work for him. Let God know you are ready and willing to follow.
- Pray for courage to stand for God when you face situations that are driven by the greed and evil of this world.

Between Sessions

Personal Reflections

Play a personal version of *Where's Waldo?* Turn back the pages of your memory to different seasons of your life and identify where God was present and at work. Look carefully, identify God's work, and give him thanks!

- When you were a little boy or girl
- In your junior high or high school years
- In your young-adult years
- In the past year

Personal Action

This week identify a "Mordecai" in your life: a family member, friend, church leader, or other person who has offered spiritual wisdom and guidance in some season of your life. Then do three things. First, lift up a prayer and thank God for placing this person in your life. Second, write, email, or call the person and express your appreciation. Third, tell someone else about this person's spiritual influence.

Read for Next Session

Take time before your next small group to read chapter 21 of *The Story*.

SESSION 21

Rebuilding the Walls

Often, when God wants something done,
he calls us to work side-by-side with each other and with him.

Introduction

Back in chapter 1 of *The Story*, God created the heavens and the earth. He placed Adam and Eve in the garden and told them to work the land and enjoy the fruit of their labors. Just think about it: before any sin or rebellion existed in the world, God gave his people jobs. In perfect paradise Adam and Eve were not going to simply hang out and do nothing; they had the joy and privilege of working.

In chapter 21 of *The Story* we see that God's pattern of calling his people to fruitful labor was still in place. God called them to rebuild the temple and reestablish worship under the leadership of Ezra. Through their hard work God would provide a beautiful place for his people to gather and worship.

Similarly, God called Nehemiah to lead the people in a massive construction project to rebuild the wall around the city and place gates back on their hinges. This job would include consistent and harsh resistance and take great courage and physical energy.

Maybe most important of all, God wanted the people to work at their relationship with him. Like all relationships, this one would demand time and effort. Indeed, all through *The Story* God is seeking to bring his people back into a healthy, intimate relationship with him.

Talk About It

Tell about your first job or a moment in life when you discovered that some things demand good old-fashioned hard work.

DVD Teaching Notes

As you watch the video segment for session 21, use the following outline to record anything that stands out to you.

Three building projects

Hearing the Word of God

Obeying the Word of God

Malachi has the last word

DVD Discussion

1. Ezra had devoted himself to studying God's Word and following what it teaches (Ezra 7:1 – 10; *The Story*, pp. 291 – 292). How did Ezra's commitment to God's Word shape his life and ministry?

   Why is it so important that we do more than just know the content of the Bible but actually obey what the Bible teaches?

2. Randy noted that throughout *The Story* God calls his people to (1) refocus on God; (2) recenter on his plan for our lives; (3) remember who God is; and (4) rebuild our relationship with him. Tell about what you have learned in the past twenty weeks about one of these four themes.

3. God worked through King Artaxerxes to send the exiles back to Jerusalem to rebuild the temple and reestablish worship (Ezra 7:11 – 28; *The Story*, pp. 293 – 294). How have you seen God use surprising people and circumstances to accomplish his will in this world?

4. Nehemiah was a man of prayer (Nehemiah 1, 4, 6; *The Story*, pp. 294–299). What situations led Nehemiah to pray and what do we learn from his example?

5. Nehemiah not only prayed hard but he worked hard. How do you see this balance in Nehemiah's life? What is the danger of praying hard but not working hard? What are some possible consequences of working hard but forgetting to pray?

6. As the people were seeking to rebuild their relationship with God, they got very serious about reading the Bible. They even had a team of people available to help everyone understand the meaning of God's Word. In what ways can we help the next generation learn to know, love, and follow the teaching of the Bible (in our homes and churches)?

The Bible is not made of 100 ancient, unrelated paintings, but a mural all knitted together to tell of God's great love for us and the extent he will go to get us back.

7. Malachi was the last prophet of the Old Testament and this movement of *The Story*. He challenged the people to give God their first and best, not their last and leftovers (Malachi 1:6–10; 3:6–12; *The Story*,

pp. 302 – 304). What are some ways we give God our leftovers rather than our first and best?

Why is it so important that we give God the first and best of all we have? What are examples of how we can do this?

8. When the people of God heard the Word of God read and had it explained to them, they moved into action. In this case, they reestablished the feast of tabernacles. Tell of a time you read the Bible and were quickly moved to action because of what God taught you.

Obeying God's Word, aligning our lives to his plan, brings joy to our lives like nothing else.

9. Read movements 1 – 5 of *The Story* (pp. 10 – 11 of this participant's guide). How do these five movements all connect together to reveal God's love for us?

Closing Prayer

As you take time to pray, here are some ideas to get you started:

- Thank God that the Bible is available and accessible today and pray that you will learn to love it and make time to study it regularly.
- Ask God to lead you to natural conversations with him and frequent prayer as you walk through the challenges of daily life.
- Ask God to help you strike a healthy balance of praying for his help and working hard to do your part.

Between Sessions

Personal Reflections

Malachi rebuked the people for giving sick animals as their offering to God and pointed out that their political leaders would never put up with such halfhearted gifts. Reflect on your own giving patterns. Ask yourself:

- Am I giving God my first and best?
- Are there ways I throw God my leftovers?
- How could I learn to give with greater joy and commitment?
- Is there any way I am robbing God by keeping for myself what is rightly his?

Personal Action

Nehemiah reminded the people of Israel of the importance of celebrating and feasting together. Plan a meal with some Christian friends for the express purpose of rejoicing in God's goodness. Read a portion of this chapter of *The Story* (Nehemiah 8:1 – 12; *The Story*, pp. 300 – 301) and let the conversation around the dinner table focus on how God has been good and why he is worthy of our worship and praise.

Read for Next Session

Take time before your next small group to read chapter 22 of *The Story*.

The Birth of the King

The journey can be adventurous, and we should enjoy it.
But let's be honest, there is something nice about finally arriving!

Introduction

From all over the United States and beyond people visit the Grand Canyon in Arizona so they can feast their eyes on one of the most amazing natural wonders on the face of this planet.

The thing about the Grand Canyon is that snapshots and videos simply don't do justice to its grandeur. Friends can try to describe it and artists can paint pictures, but nothing compares with actually breathing in the beauty and breathtaking majesty of it all.

If you have made this pilgrimage you might have vivid memories of kids in the backseat asking, for the hundredth time, "Are we there yet?" Then, finally, as the moment arrives, all the hours of travel seem like nothing as you stand on the edge of the sheer drop-off and your eyes span the chasm. An almost holy hush falls over those you have traveled with ... you stand in awe!

For the past 21 chapters of *The Story* we have been on the journey, wondering when we will get there. Today we have arrived. We look into the manger and behold the Lord of Glory, "God with us," the long-awaited Messiah.

Let a holy hush fall over your heart. Look closely. This is the One who made the Grand Canyon, the heavens and the earth ... and everything in them. God in a manger. We have arrived!

Talk About It

Tell about a time you traveled a long way to see someone or something and describe how it felt when you finally arrived.

DVD Teaching Notes

As you watch the video segment for session 22, use the following outline to record anything that stands out to you.

Lower Story: scandalous beginnings

Upper Story: God's solution to our scandalous beginnings

God comes down to bring us back to himself

The fulfillment of many prophecies

DVD Discussion

1. Do you remember the first few words of the first chapter of *The Story*? If not, turn back and read them ... then, read the start of this chapter. The Jews in Jesus' day had read and heard the story over and over through their lives. What would have come to their minds when the story of Jesus (the solution to all our problems) began with the same words that started *The Story*, back before there was any sin in the world?

2. Various titles and descriptions of Jesus are included in his story (John 1:1 – 14; *The Story*, pp. 309 – 310). Pick one of the following and explain what you think it means and how you have experienced this to be true of Jesus:

   Jesus: The Word
   Jesus: Is God
   Jesus: The Maker of all things
   Jesus: The Life
   Jesus: The Light
   Jesus: The one and only Son
   Jesus: The one who brings grace and truth

3. God spoke to both Mary and Joseph through angels (Luke 1:26 – 38; Matthew 1:19 – 24; *The Story*, pp. 310 – 312). What was the angel's message and how did Mary and Joseph respond to this heavenly messenger?

Jesus' birth is not the result of a scandal ... but a solution to our scandal—our sin.

4. Pause to remember that Mary and Joseph were real people living in a real small town. How might Joseph's family and the townspeople have responded when Mary turned up pregnant before the wedding day? How might they have reacted to the "An angel told me that God would make me pregnant, but Joseph and I are still virgins" story?

   Tell about a time that God called you to live for him or follow him in a way that others did not understand. How did you hold to your faith during this time?

5. Jesus was born of a virgin and was conceived without sin. Why does this matter?

> *From the Lower Story it looked like this baby would be born in sin, but from the Upper Story we see that Jesus was born without sin.*

6. In the Lower Story Joseph and Mary had to go to Bethlehem to be counted in the census; it was a hard three-day journey for someone nine months pregnant. In the Upper Story God was getting them to Bethlehem because that is where the Messiah was to be born. Recall an event in your life that seemed inconvenient and unnecessary, only to later look back and realize God was doing something greater than you knew at the time.

7. After Jesus was born, the shepherds hurried off and told everyone what they had seen and heard. Share a brief testimony about a time you really saw or heard Jesus move in your life. How might you share this story (and others like it) outside your small group ... with people who are not yet followers of Jesus?

8. Jesus is Immanuel, "God with us" (Matthew 1:23; *The Story*, p. 312). As you walk with Jesus your Savior, how does it help you to know that he is God and that he is with you ... all the time?

   In what situation do you need to be reminded that God is with you? How can your small group members pray for you as you walk through this season of your life?

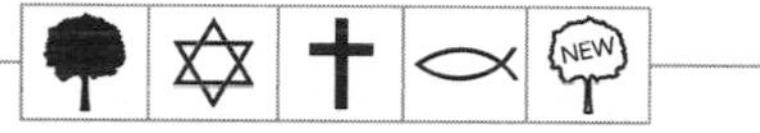

9. Read movements 1–5 of *The Story* (pp. 10–11 of this participant's guide). How do you see God's compassion and justice at work as you grow to understand the scope of his story?

Closing Prayer

As you take time to pray, here are some ideas to get you started:

- Thank God that his Upper Story work is always the right thing, even when we don't fully understand what he is doing.
- Pray for courage to follow God, even when it is hard.
- Pray for eyes to see Jesus as he is: the Light, the Life, Immanuel, the Son of God, God, the Savior, and so much more!

Between Sessions

Personal Reflections

If we could really get hold of the truth of being freed from our sins, we would be filled with unspeakable joy. Thank God for sending his Son to pay the price of your sins. Praise Jesus for the great love he demonstrated by sacrificing himself on the cross.

Personal Action

At the end of the DVD segment, Randy talked about how Jesus wants to do three distinct things in and through us. In the coming week pray about and then identify one action you can take to grow in each of these three areas:

- Jesus wants to come in you. (Invite him to dwell fully in you by his Spirit.)
- He wants to grow in you. (Pray that you will go deeper and deeper in faith.)
- He wants to come out of you. (Ask Jesus to let his light shine through you and touch the lives of others.)

Read for Next Session

Take time before your next small group to read chapter 23 of *The Story.*

SESSION 23

Jesus' Ministry Begins

God's solution for our sin problem
is not a "What" but a "Who."

Introduction

Religion is always about "What." What am I supposed to do? What should I stop doing? What clothes should I wear? What words can't I say anymore? What will people think of me? And the hit parade of "Whats" just keeps going!

By chapter 23 of *The Story* the people of Israel had compiled a massive list of "Whats" in an attempt to please God and show that they were worthy of his love and acceptance. Some religious leaders of that day had become experts in telling everyone else what they were supposed to do.

Into this climate God breaks in with his Upper Story and surprises everyone. Salvation is not based on a list of what we do to make God happy and what we won't do because it is against the rules. Of course, God cares about our behavior and wants his children to grow in holiness, but this is not his first concern. Before we begin thinking about being good people, we need to meet the One who can help us become good.

The solution to the problem, way back in the first century, was not a "What" but a "Who." It was all about Jesus. Now, two thousand years later, it is exactly the same. Before we begin thinking about the "What," we need to meet the "Who." He is still Jesus!

Talk About It

Some people today still think salvation is about a list of do's and don'ts. When people head down this road, what are some things they put on the "What we have to do" list and the "What we can't do" list?

DVD Teaching Notes

As you watch the video segment for session 23, use the following outline to record anything that stands out to you.

John the Baptist introduces us to God's solution

Jesus is the Lamb of God

Encounters that teach us Jesus is the "Who" we have been waiting for

John the Baptist dies knowing who Jesus is

DVD Discussion

1. At the baptism of Jesus (Matthew 3:13–17; *The Story*, p. 322), what did the people see and hear and how did this clarify who Jesus was?

> *John the Baptist tells us that the solution to our problem is not a "What" but a "Who." We have to understand who he is before we can understand what he came to do. What he is going to do will only make a difference if he is who he says he is.*

2. After forty days in the wilderness Jesus faced three temptations from the devil (Matthew 4:1–11; *The Story*, pp. 322–323). What was each temptation and what did Jesus say to fend off each? How does Satan use similar types of temptation in our lives today?

3. How can knowing Scripture help us battle against daily temptations? Tell about a time you used Scripture to stand strong against the enemy.

4. Chapter 4 of *The Story* told of the Passover lamb (Exodus 12:1–30; *The Story*, pp. 51–52) which was slain and whose blood was placed on the doorpost to protect God's people in Egypt from the angel of death. Now

John the Baptist calls Jesus "the Lamb of God, who takes away the sins of the world" (John 1:29; *The Story*, p. 323). First-century Jews knew all about the Passover and the sacrificial system. What message would John's words about Jesus have sent them and what message should it send us today?

> *Jesus is the Lamb of God. No Jewish person could have misunderstood what John was saying. The young, unblemished, innocent lamb of the Old Testament was the one whose life was given up and whose blood was shed to pay for sins.*

5. As Jesus called people to follow him, many immediately invited someone else to meet the Savior. Who has God placed in your life that you would like to invite to know Jesus? How can your group members pray for you as you seek to reach out to this person with God's love and grace?

6. In Jesus' encounter with Nicodemus (John 3:1 – 21; *The Story*, pp. 326 – 327), Jesus talked about the Upper Story while Nicodemus focused on the Lower Story. How do you see these two stories conflicting in their conversation? How did Jesus help Nicodemus think in Upper Story terms?

What does Jesus reveal to Nicodemus and to us about the heart of God, heaven, and judgment in this passage?

7. Jesus told the woman at the well that God looks for people who will worship the Father in Spirit and in truth (John 4:21 – 24; *The Story*, p. 328). What helps you connect with God's Holy Spirit? What helps you grow more authentic and truthful as you worship?

8. Jesus sought out quiet places where he could meet with the Father face-to-face (Mark 1:35; *The Story*, p. 330). Why is it important that Christians today make regular time to be quiet before God? How are you doing in this area and how can your group members support you in this discipline of spiritual growth?

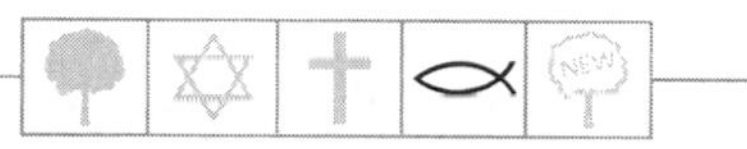

9. Read movement 4 of *The Story* (pp. 11 of this participant's guide). If one of your group members has memorized this short statement that describes the heartbeat of the fourth movement, allow them to quote it and tell about what God taught them as they committed this statement to memory.

Closing Prayer

As you take time to pray, here are some ideas to get you started:

- Pray that we will recognize Jesus in our midst, throughout each day of our lives.
- Ask God to help you notice when his Upper Story is breaking into your life.
- Praise Jesus for coming as our Messiah and the Savior of the world.

Between Sessions

Personal Reflections

It really is all about the "Who." Spend time reflecting on who Jesus is, letting the stories in this chapter guide you. What do you learn about Jesus as you:

- Watch him being baptized
- Listen to John the Baptist talk about him
- See him calling followers
- Listen to his conversation with Nicodemus
- Hear the woman at the well talk with him
- See him heal the sick and cast out demons
- Consider how he dealt with the religious leaders of his day

Personal Action

When Jesus called Levi (Matthew) to follow him, new relational bridges were built (Mark 2:13 – 17; *The Story*, p. 331). Matthew invited Jesus to his house for a party and also invited all his "old friends," who happened to be tax collectors, prostitutes, and sinners.

When Christians invite committed believers and nonbelievers to a place where they can connect relationally, good things can happen. Consider planning a party or dinner and invite both committed Christians and spiritual seekers. Pray for God to do great things ... and see what he does.

Read for Next Session

Take time before your next small group to read chapter 24 of *The Story.*

SESSION 24

No Ordinary Man

Some people might call reading,
writing, and arithmetic the fundamentals,
but when Jesus entered the classroom of history,
he taught what matters most of all.

Introduction

A pastor once had a man in his congregation who would from time to time approach him after the message and, with a twinkle in his eye, say, "Well, Pastor, as you got into your message today, the battery in my hearing aid died."

This was code for "I stopped listening when you hit on a topic (giving, holiness, humble service) that I did not want to hear." Apparently, the man had a bad case of Intentional Selective Hearing (ISH). Sadly, he missed out on truth that would have made his life better and drawn him closer to the Savior.

Even in Jesus' day the crowds, religious leaders, and sometimes the disciples themselves suffered from this sickness. They would ignore or even reject what Jesus said.

Two thousand years later, the teaching of Jesus can still be so piercing, convicting, and painfully true that we intentionally, or unintentionally, shut it off. As his followers, we must resist the occasional bout of ISH and cling to every word of the Savior ... even when those words challenge us to the core of our being.

Talk About It

Tell of a time when you read something in the Bible, heard a sermon, or had God bring a truth to your heart that you initially felt like rejecting or disobeying. What helped you finally come to a place where you accepted or embraced that truth?

DVD Teaching Notes

As you watch the video segment for session 24, use the following outline to record anything that stands out to you.

Jesus is the Master Teacher

Jesus taught in parables

Jesus taught directly

Jesus taught through life experiences

DVD Discussion

1. What are some ways we can really tune in and open our hearts, ready to receive the truth God wants to speak in our life?

> *Jesus is the Master Teacher ... teaching us how to align our lives in the Lower Story according to God's Upper Story plan.*

2. In one of Jesus' most famous parables he used agricultural language and imagery to teach powerful spiritual truths (Mark 4:1 – 20; *The Story*, pp. 335 – 336). What are the four different kinds of soil in this parable and what do they represent?

   How can these same things still get in the way of people receiving God's truth and hearing his message?

3. Jesus told three parables about lost things that were found (Luke 15; *The Story*, pp. 337 – 339). What similar threads run through these stories and what do you learn about the love and heart of God from them?

4. Jesus taught with stories but also in more traditional messages, such as the Sermon on the Mount, where he called his followers to be salt and light (Matthew 5:13 – 16; *The Story*, p. 341). What was he getting at with this challenge and how can we be salt and light in our daily lives?

5. Jesus taught his followers how to pray, the so-called "Lord's Prayer" (Matthew 6:9 – 15; *The Story*, p. 341). This prayer was not given as a set of words to be repeated over and over with no thought to their meaning. Instead, each line was meant as a springboard to lead us through key areas of concern. What themes does Jesus call us to include in our prayers and how can his words move us to a deeper place of prayer?

We are hungry, need daily bread, hold grudges, and experience stumbles into temptation. This is the Lower Story. So, we cry out to God to meet us in our Lower Story, and he does.

6. Randy noted a third way that Jesus taught: using real-life situations as occasions to communicate deep spiritual truth. Why are real-life situations a good way to teach, particularly for parents and grandparents?

7. What lesson did Jesus teach after Peter tried to walk on the water (Matthew 14:22 – 33; *The Story*, pp. 348 – 349), and how can we learn from this lesson today?

8. Jesus is the Master Teacher, and that makes every Christian a student. What is one area of your life in which you feel God wants you to become a humble student and receive the teaching of Jesus?

9. Read movement 5 of *The Story* (p. 11 of this participant's guide). How does the hope of heaven help you understand God's work in your life today?

Closing Prayer

Using the Lord's Prayer to guide you, pray through these themes:

- Lift up God for who he is, in his holiness. Declare his many names.
- Pray that his kingdom will come.
- Pray that his will be done in your life and on earth.
- Ask for his provision of what you need — daily bread.
- Ask for forgiveness and for power to forgive others.
- Pray that he will deliver you from temptation and give strength to resist.
- Pray against the wiles and tactics of the devil.

Between Sessions

Personal Reflections

Some of the best lessons Christians learn come from godly older people who have simply taught us in the natural flow of life. This is exactly what God had in mind in Deuteronomy 6:4 – 9 when he told the people to talk about his truth with their children at home, as they were taking walks, in the morning and in the evening. Consider how you can naturally share the truth of God's Word in normal daily interactions with the next generation.

Personal Action

Jesus told stories about a lost coin, a lost sheep, and a lost son. In each case, when the lost thing was found, a celebration followed. The message is this: a person coming to faith in Jesus ignites a party in heaven. Plan a party with some Christian friends for the express purpose of celebrating the fact that you are followers of Jesus. Take turns sharing how God brought you to faith and the people he used in the process. You might want to read Luke 15 at the party.

Read for Next Session

Take time before your next small group to read chapter 25 of *The Story*.

SESSION 25

Jesus, the Son of God

Everyone seems to have a theory on who Jesus was . . .
only Jesus has the real answer.

Introduction

Sometime in the 1960s and '70s a new kind of thinking arose and specific language came with it. People started "trying to find themselves." Men and women would begin a personal quest to discover who they were. Young people would drop out of school so they could figure themselves out. Middle-agers, men in particular, would go through a midlife crisis, struggling with their identity and purpose.

Certainly in Jesus' day, most people did not have the luxury of "finding themselves." But they did enjoy coming up with theories about who Jesus was ... his true identity. The only one who was crystal clear about the answer to this question was Jesus himself. While people guessed, suggested, and made innuendos, Jesus waited for the right moment to declare publicly what he had known from before time.

Jesus always knew his identity and mission. At the right time, he made it clear, so that we would have the right answer to the question, "Who is Jesus?"

Talk About It

If you were to survey people walking down the street of a major city, what are some of the responses you would get to the question, "Who is Jesus?"

DVD Teaching Notes

As you watch the video segment for session 25, use the following outline to record anything that stands out to you.

Jesus asks, "Who do people say I am?"

Peter responds

The religious leaders and others respond

Jesus declares his true identity

DVD Discussion

1. In an encounter with Peter, Jesus gave the Son of Man's job description (Mark 8:31 – 33; *The Story*, p. 353). What things did Jesus say he would do and how did Peter respond? Why do you think Peter responded as he did?

   Jesus' response to Peter was very strong! What had Peter done wrong and how was Jesus' response an act of love?

2. Jesus told his followers they would do four things as they walked with him day by day: (1) deny self, (2) take up his cross, (3) follow him, and (4) be willing to lay down their lives for him and the gospel. What does it look like, in an ordinary day of your life, for you to seek to do these things?

3. God declared who Jesus is and what we are called to do in response (Matthew 17:5; *The Story*, p. 354). In what ways can we live out this calling on a daily basis?

4. Human kings in the Bible (and in our world today) were exalted and received special honor. When Jesus walked on this earth he acted very differently. What contrasts do you see between how Jesus lived and how other kings live and behave?

5. When Jesus called himself the "light of the world," he assured his disciples that they would no longer walk in the dark if they followed him. How have you discovered the light of Jesus since you became a Christian and how does his presence keep you from living in the darkness?

6. As Jesus interacted with some of the religious elite he declared, "Before Abraham was born, I am!" (John 8:58; *The Story*, p. 358). What was Jesus claiming and why did this upset the religious leaders so much that they wanted to kill him?

Jesus is the Lamb, without blemish,
that died a million times
in all those sacrifices in Israel.
He is God. He is the Lamb of God
offered up for our sins.

7. Lazarus was sick, so his sisters sent word to Jesus (John 11; *The Story*, pp. 358 – 359). In this encounter Jesus declared that he was "the resurrection and life." What was Jesus claiming about himself and why did it matter at that time and today?

8. Jesus is the Savior, Messiah, and Lamb of God. He came to live a sinless life, die on the cross in our place, and rise again in glory to break the power of sin and death. How does the truth of his identity clarify your life purpose and direction?

NEW

9. Read movement 5 of *The Story* (p. 11 of this participant's guide). If one of your group members has memorized this short statement that describes the heartbeat of the fifth movement, allow them to quote it and tell about what God taught them as they committed this statement to memory.

> *We now know God's full plan. He sent his Son, who sat by his side in the Upper Story to come down to the Lower Story to represent us. God's plan was for him to die. He paid for our sins so we could be made right with God and come back into a personal relationship with him like Adam and Eve had.*

Closing Prayer

As you take time to pray, here are some ideas to get you started:

- Pray for people in your community, nation, and the world to get a clear picture of who Jesus really is.
- Ask Jesus to set the course of your life direction based on who he is, not who you are.
- Declare that Jesus is the resurrection and the life and thank him for the hope of heaven that belongs to all who believe in him.

Between Sessions

Personal Reflections

Jesus came to be the perfect and final sacrifice for our sins. Reflect on what you have been saved from. Praise God for cleansing you of all sin because the Messiah, Jesus, paid the price in full.

Personal Action

As we walk through life we meet people who have all sorts of theories on who Jesus is. Make a commitment to read the Gospels (Matthew, Mark, Luke, and John) and keep a journal of all the things Jesus said about himself. Then ask the Holy Spirit to help you gently and graciously paint an accurate portrayal of Jesus to those people you encounter who have misconceptions about him.

Read for Next Session

Take time before your next small group to read chapter 26 of *The Story*.

SESSION 26

The Hour of Darkness

His darkest hour
led to our brightest!

Introduction

No moment in all history depicts a greater contrast between the Upper and Lower Story. The final week of Jesus' life, in the Lower Story, was as dark as darkness gets. The Lord of Glory was betrayed and abandoned by his friends, rejected by the crowds, condemned by the religious community, scorned and mocked mercilessly. He experienced absolute relational and emotional darkness.

The one humbly born in a manger was strung up on a post and brutally beaten. He was forced to carry his own cross up the hill of the Skull. Then he was nailed to that Roman instrument of torture and suspended up in the air by his hands and feet — suffering one of the most intentionally painful deaths ever invented. He experienced physical darkness beyond description.

Finally, the sinless Lamb of God experienced the pitch-blackness of utter spiritual darkness. The one who knew no sin became sin; in our place he took the punishment, the just judgment, we deserved.

Strangely, this darkest of all moments was also the moment heavenly light broke through as never before. As Jesus suffered and died, our hope began, our redemption was won, and sin was crushed. The brilliant light of God's love was shining from the glory of the Upper Story into the darkness of our Lower Story ... and it changed everything.

Talk About It

Tell about a time you experienced relational, emotional, or spiritual darkness and how the light of God was still shining.

DVD Teaching Notes

As you watch the video segment for session 26, use the following outline to record anything that stands out to you.

Jesus, the sinless Son of God, provides the way back to God

In the Lower Story they said, "He is finished!"

In the Upper Story Jesus said, "It is finished!"

A new beginning

DVD Discussion

1. As Jesus prepared for the Passover meal (a time laden with imagery of sacrificed lambs and shed blood) he did not stop teaching and showing his followers how to live (John 13:1 – 17; *The Story*, pp. 367 – 368). Describe the act of service Jesus offered his disciples (including Judas) and how they responded.

   How does our willingness to serve reveal Jesus' presence in our life and in the world? What is one unexpected act of service you can offer in the coming week?

2. Jesus was emphatically clear that he is the only way back to a restored relationship with the Father, the only path to heaven (John 14:6; *The Story*, p. 370). How do some people (even Christians) push back on this exclusive claim of Jesus? Why is it important for us to embrace this clear teaching of the Savior?

3. Right before his arrest, Jesus took three of his friends and went to a garden to pray (Matthew 26:36 – 46; *The Story*, pp. 372 – 373). What do you learn about the love and power of God, contrasted with the weakness and need of people, as you read this account?

4. The religious leaders and the political leaders joined in a twisted tale of abuse and rejection (Matthew 26:57 – 67; 27:1 – 10; John 18:28 – 19:16; *The Story*, pp. 374 – 377). How did they treat Jesus and how did he respond?

> *When Jesus died, the leaders of the Lower Story proclaimed, "He is finished." But Jesus from the Upper Story said, "It is finished."*

5. Peter, one of Jesus' closest friends, vigorously denied three times that he even knew the Lord — even as Jesus watched on (Luke 22:54 – 62; *The Story*, p. 375). How must this have felt to Jesus? What are ways we deny Jesus and act like we don't know him?

6. What do you learn about the heart of Jesus as he hung on the cross (Luke 23:32 – 43; John 19:25 – 27; *The Story*, pp. 378 – 379), interacting with those who crucified him, the thief who reached out to him, and his own mother?

7. One of the briefest, most powerful statements in all of *The Story* is when Jesus said, "It is finished." From a Lower Story perspective, what must people have thought when Jesus spoke these words? From an Upper

Story spiritual reality, what was Jesus declaring and what does this mean for us?

8. Hebrews 10:19–22, the passage Randy read in the DVD segment, points out three things that happen when we enter a friendship with Jesus. How have you experienced (or how are you experiencing) *one* of these in your life:
   - We can draw near God with absolute confidence
   - We no longer have a guilty conscience
   - We live with a sense of being cleansed and pure

   What can we do on a daily basis to walk in an intimate and living friendship with God?

> *Through the shed blood of Christ, we now have direct access to God. The curse of Adam has been lifted for all who believe in Jesus as the Son of God, the Messiah. Finally the way back to God has come. The only thing left for us to do is to reach and receive it for ourselves.*

9. Read movements 1–5 of *The Story* (pp. 10–11 of this participant's guide). How is God's power and presence in the Upper Story impacting what happens in the Lower Story?

Closing Prayer

As you take time to pray, here are some ideas to get you started:

- Thank Jesus for loving you so much that he would experience utter darkness as your sins and judgment became his.
- Praise God for sending his Holy Spirit to be with us and in us. Ask the Spirit to fill you to overflowing.
- In the garden, Jesus told his followers to pray that they would not fall into temptation. Pray against the lures and enticements the enemy puts in your path.

Between Sessions

Personal Reflections

Read Hebrews 10:19 – 22 and meditate on the truths that God has opened the way for you to draw near him with confidence, that you can live with a clear conscience through the sacrifice of Jesus, and that you have been washed and cleansed. Rejoice in these truths.

Personal Action

The whole purpose of Jesus entering the Lower Story and offering himself as a sacrifice was to bring us back into relationship with God. Write a brief account of how the death of Jesus has personally changed your life. Then share this brief reflection with a friend or two, and maybe with your pastor.

Read for Next Session

Take time before your next small group to read chapter 27 of *The Story.*

SESSION 27

The Resurrection

Up to this point in history it could be said,
"Out of death comes death."
Now a new message rings loud and clear,
"Out of death comes life!"

Introduction

Do you remember playing with a Jack-in-the-Box as a child? You would turn a crank on the side of this small metal toy (usually as the tune "Here We Go 'Round the Mulberry Bush" kept time with your movement). As the song neared the end, you would slow your cranking and begin to wince. You knew what was coming. You had done this a hundred times before. But there was still a sense of odd anticipation.

All of a sudden, with a slight rotation of the crank, the top of the box would flip open with a loud snap, and a spring-loaded head would pop up. Every single time Jack popped out of the box, you would be startled. But then you would press Jack's head down, click the lid of the box shut, and begin cranking again.

As we read chapter 27 of *The Story,* we watch the disciples respond with stunned amazement at the resurrection of Jesus. He had told them, repeatedly, that he would die and rise again on the third day. He had assured them that death could not hold him down. But when Jesus popped out of the grave, the disciples were as shocked as a child with a Jack-in-the-Box!

Talk About It

Tell about something you knew was going to happen, but were still surprised and amazed when it actually did.

DVD Teaching Notes

As you watch the video segment for session 27, use the following outline to record anything that stands out to you.

The disciples feel the sting of the Lower Story

An empty tomb: he is risen

Resurrection appearances

Jesus commissions his followers before returning to the Upper Story

DVD Discussion

1. Tell about a person you were close with who has passed away. How is that person's life still impacting yours?

2. Mary stood outside the empty tomb weeping ... until Jesus revealed himself to her (John 20:10 – 18; *The Story*, pp. 383 – 384). What did Jesus teach her about himself? Tell about a moment when your eyes were opened, with greater clarity, and you came to know Jesus in a deeper way than you had before that moment.

> *Jesus is not finished. He is alive. But his work is finished. The way has been made open for all people, all nations, just as he promised Abraham, to receive the blessing of eternal life with God.*

3. On the road to Emmaus the resurrected Jesus taught two men the truth of the Old Testament Scriptures (Luke 24:13 – 49; *The Story*, pp. 384 – 386). How does understanding the first part of *The Story* (the Old Testament) help us understand the rest of it (the New Testament)?

4. Thomas was not willing to believe Jesus was alive until he saw him with his own eyes (John 20:24–29; *The Story*, p. 386). When Jesus revealed himself to Thomas, how did he seek to meet Thomas right where he was and help him move toward faith? How has God met you similarly?

5. The risen Jesus met the disciples while they were out fishing (John 21:1–19; *The Story*, pp. 386–388). How did Peter respond when he realized it was Jesus? What did Jesus do to restore Peter and set him back on course to live a life of service?

   At the end of Jesus' interaction with Peter, he said, "Follow me!" the same words he spoke when he first called Peter. Tell how Jesus has called you to follow him and one way you are seeking to live out this calling.

6. Before Jesus ascended back to the Upper Story of heaven, he called his followers to specific tasks (Matthew 28:16–20; *The Story*, p. 388). What did Jesus call them (and us) to do and what is God's part and our part in this mission?

7. Where in your life are you feeling the sting of Lower Story pain but also experiencing Upper Story joy? How does focusing on Jesus' resurrection and the assurance of our own bring hope and strength in life's tough times?

8. When we understand the message of *The Story* and enter a restored relationship with God, we want to share it with others. Who is one person you are praying will enter a relationship with Jesus and how are you seeking to reach out to him or her? How can your group members encourage you in this relationship and support you in prayer?

---

9. Scan movements 1 – 5 of *The Story* (pp. 10 – 11 of this participant's guide). Tell group members which movement has best helped you understand God's passionate heart for people who are wandering far from him. As you do this, read or recite the words of that movement to the group.

> *We will no longer have to stand before the gravesides of people we have loved and grieve with no hope. If they embrace this free gift of forgiveness for themselves, they too will not be finished. We will see each other again in the garden of God to come.*

Closing Prayer

As you take time to pray, here are some ideas to get you started:

- Thank God for people you love who have passed away but still influence your walk of faith because of their great example.
- After the resurrection some people had a hard time recognizing Jesus. Ask the Holy Spirit to open your eyes to see Jesus with clarity.
- Pray that God will use you in his mission to make disciples of all nations.

Between Sessions

Personal Reflections

A Christian's funeral is filled with the hope and assurance of a glorious future. Not so for funerals of those who do not know Christ. Reflect on the people you love who do not have a relationship with Jesus. Invite God to direct how you might become more involved in their lives.

Personal Action

Create a list of the people you love and care about who have not discovered the truth of God's story and who are not yet in a relationship with God through faith in Jesus. Commit to use this list as a prayer reminder. Also, seek opportunities to share God's story and your story with them. Consider giving them a copy of *The Story* and encourage them to read it.

Read for Next Session

Take time before your next small group to read chapter 28 of *The Story*.

SESSION 28

New Beginnings

The human heart longs
for a fresh start and a new vision.
In Jesus we have received
the new beginning our soul longs for.

Introduction

"It's nice to share our toys!" That's what parents in every generation tell their little children. Some kids get the message and others don't seem to catch on.

Teenagers face the same challenge. "Let someone else use the remote control and pick the TV show." "Don't grab the last piece of pizza."

Fortunately, people become generous and share naturally by the time they enter the grown-up world ... right? Wrong! It is still a battle and a challenge, well into our adult years.

In chapter 28 of *The Story* we hear our heavenly Father say, "It's nice to share!" God tells his people that the grace they have received, the love they are experiencing, the amazing fellowship they share as a community of believers, the forgiveness of sins, and the restored relationship they have with God should not be hoarded and kept hidden. God calls his people, then and now, to share the good news and hope found in Jesus alone.

How are we doing? Are we quick to share? Have we discovered that the more we give away the things of God, the more we have?

Talk About It

Describe a time when you had something brand new and found it difficult to share with others.

DVD Teaching Notes

As you watch the video segment for session 28, use the following outline to record anything that stands out to you.

From creation to the resurrection ... God's plan to restore us

The presence and power of the Holy Spirit

Revival and the birth of a new community

What the early believers did when they gathered

DVD Discussion

1. In the DVD segment, Randy gave a snapshot of the gospel and reminded us that if we believe that Jesus was God among us, lived a sinless life, died for our sins, and rose again, we can become children of God. How did you learn this truth and who did God use to share it with you?

2. Jesus was clear that our source of power to share his life-saving message is the Holy Spirit (Acts 1:8; *The Story*, p. 389). Indeed, the people experienced this when the Spirit came on them (Acts 2:1–4; *The Story*, p. 390); likewise, Peter was filled with the Spirit and proclaimed the message with boldness (Acts 2:14–40; *The Story*, pp. 391–392). How have you experienced the Holy Spirit filling you, moving you, and giving you strength to share the message and love of Jesus?

The Spirit is going to dwell in the lives of all believers in Jesus. His presence will give the disciples the courage, guidance, and power to pull off their new mission.

3. Jesus told his followers that their ministry would occur in four distinct locations (Acts 1:8; *The Story*, p. 389). How do you see God using you, your church, and the church at large to share the life-saving message of Jesus in each of the following places:
   - Jerusalem (your hometown/neighborhood)
   - Judea (your surrounding community and region)
   - Samaria (the tough places that many people avoid)
   - The ends of the earth (around the nation and world)

   How could your group members team up to get involved in sharing the love, grace, and message of Jesus in one of these places?

4. Along with sharing the message and love of Jesus, we are also called to share our resources/material goods, our meals/fellowship, and our lives/stories. How is each valuable and what can we do to share these more intentionally?

> *Out of the overflow of their lives together, they began to meet the needs of each other and the people around them. Their offer of care was different. It was unconditional.*

5. What sorts of conflict and spiritual battle did the early Christians face as they tried to share Jesus' message? How did they respond to persecution and resistance and how can this inspire us as we encounter people who push back against the message of God's love?

6. Peter (Acts 4:8 – 12; *The Story*, p. 394), Stephen (Acts 6:8 – 15; 7:51 – 60; *The Story*, pp. 397 – 399), and later the apostle Paul were clear that Jesus Christ was the Messiah, the only hope for salvation. How did people respond to that bold claim in the religiously diverse ancient world and how do they respond today? How do we continue sharing with boldness, even when others disagree with us?

7. Three thousand people came to faith in Jesus at Pentecost and their ranks swelled in succeeding days. Is your local church seeing regular conversions and lives changed by Jesus? If so, how can you celebrate and encourage this? If not, what steps can you take to help your church reach out more effectively with the life-saving love and message of Jesus?

8. The risen Jesus called his followers to be his witnesses. Give an example of how we can share the message of the gospel in *one* of the following ways:
   - By sharing the story of Jesus
   - By sharing the story of when we placed our faith in the Savior
   - By sharing specific stories about the presence and power of Jesus at work in our life today

Jesus told us over and over again that if we will acknowledge him for who he is and will acknowledge our sin and accept his gift as full payment we can become children of God. This is called "the gospel" or "the good news."

9. Scan movements 1 – 5 of *The Story* (pp. 10 – 11 of this participant's guide). Tell group members which movement has best helped you understand God's patience and long-suffering love. As you do this, read or recite the words of that movement to the group.

Closing Prayer

As you take time to pray, here are some ideas to get you started:

- Pray for boldness and clarity as you share the good news of Jesus with others.
- Ask for God to help you grow in generosity as you learn to share the resources he has put in your care.
- Pray for God to build your small group into a place where real community and grace are extended freely.

Between Sessions

Personal Reflections

Reflect this week on the people who shared the gospel of Jesus with you. What did they say? How did their lives reinforce the message of God's great love? Seek to use their examples as inspiration as you share the grace and the good news of Jesus with those you encounter each day.

Personal Action

The early Christians loved to open their homes for meals with others. In the coming weeks, make two invitations. First, invite a few Christians over for a meal and a time of sharing life and faith. Second, invite a few people you care about who are not yet followers of Jesus and have them share a meal with you and some of your Christian friends.

Read for Next Session

Take time before your next small group to read chapter 29 of *The Story*.

SESSION 29

Paul's Mission

Once we have the message
it is time for our mission.

Introduction

As children, most of us enjoyed connect-the-dot activity books. In the simplest books you could tell the end result before you drew a single line—a duck, a puppy, a tree ... pretty basic stuff. For older kids, the objects became more complex. As you looked at the page all you saw was a bunch of numbered dots, but you had no idea what you would discover until you had taken a pencil or marker and connected them all.

The fun of a connect-the-dots experience is the "aha!" moment. At some point, when enough of the dots have been joined by lines, you can see the finished product. Something that was unclear comes into focus.

As we read chapter 29 of *The Story*, things are becoming clear. God is connecting the dots! His plan to bring us back to himself has been realized in Jesus' death and resurrection. Now, the message of hope was being spread all over the world, particularly through the apostle Paul, who had an intentional commitment to communicate this wonderful message of Jesus.

The question is: Can we connect the dots to the modern world? Do we see that Paul's mission is really the mission of Jesus for every generation? When we do, we learn that it is our mission ... right where God has placed us today.

Talk About It

What is one way you, your family, or your church family is seeking to fulfill God's mission to bring the love and message of Jesus to your community and the world?

DVD Teaching Notes

As you watch the video segment for session 29, use the following outline to record anything that stands out to you.

Paul takes the message of salvation to the "ends of the earth"

Paul's three missionary journeys

Paul's obedience to bring the gospel to all people

Our obedience to continue the journey

DVD Discussion

1. One message that Paul brought as he proclaimed the gospel is that heaven is our true home and, in Christ, our resurrection is sure. How does a daily awareness that heaven awaits all those who have faith in Jesus bring hope, encouragement, and confidence to live for God today?

2. As Paul preached the message of Jesus, he faced spiritual attack (Acts 13:1 – 12; 16:16 – 34; *The Story*, pp. 407 – 408, 412 – 413). What form did these battles take?

   What spiritual battles might we face as we seek to bring the message and hope of Jesus to our world? How can we resist and overcome?

3. As the early church connected the dots and began spreading the life-saving message of Jesus, the truth of the gospel was declared again and again. What is the heartbeat of the gospel in each of these presentations:
   - As Paul preached to the people in Pisidian Antioch (Acts 13:13 – 39; *The Story*, pp. 408 – 409)
   - As Paul wrote to the church at Rome (Romans 1:16 – 17; Romans 3 – 6; *The Story*, pp. 432 – 434)

If a close friend or family member came to you and said, "I have watched your life and listened to your words and I want what you have. What must I believe and do to be saved?" what would you share with them?

> *The gospel has come to us because Paul was obedient to be the first to bring it to us. He courageously took up the Upper Story call of God on his life.*

4. Paul and his companions not only faced spiritual attack but also resistance from the religious and business communities (Acts 19:8 – 10, 23 – 41; *The Story*, pp. 421 – 423). How did they face both while they ministered in Ephesus? What are some ways we might face the same sort of resistance as we follow Jesus today?

5. As Paul wrote to the believers in Corinth, he addressed the problem of division in the church (1 Corinthians 1:10 – 13; 3:1 – 11; *The Story*, pp. 424 – 425). What was the issue there and how can the church today guard against similar assaults by Satan?

6. The church is a body, and every member is a specific part with a specific function (1 Corinthians 12; *The Story*, pp. 426 – 427). What is one spiritual gift God has given you and how are you developing it and using it

for his glory? How can your group members encourage you as you seek to use your gifts to serve Jesus?

7. Which of "the fruit of the Spirit" that Paul listed (Galatians 5:22 – 23; *The Story*, p. 431) do you desire to see grow in your life? How can your group members pray as you seek maturity in this area?

8. One of the great blessings of receiving Jesus is that we become children of God (Romans 8:14 – 17; *The Story*, p. 435). What does it mean to say, "I am a child of God?" How does your relationship with God grow and change when you learn to see yourself in this way?

9. Scan movements 1 – 5 of *The Story* (pp. 10 – 11 of this participant's guide). Tell group members which movement has best helped you understand God's desire to be in relationship with you. As you do this, read or recite the words of that movement to the group.

God told Abraham that it would be through his offspring that all nations would be blessed. Jesus is that offspring and Paul is the deliverer of the promise to the nations beyond Israel.

Closing Prayer

As you take time to pray, here are some ideas to get you started:

- Pray for the fruit of the Holy Spirit to grow in your life.
- Ask for strength to resist the spiritual attacks that come at those who stand up for Jesus in this world.
- Thank God for being your Abba and for giving you a loving church family filled with brothers and sisters.

Between Sessions

Personal Reflections

In this session's DVD segment, Randy pointed out that the worst that could happen to most of us if we share Jesus is a verbal rejection. Think about what hard things might happen if you become bolder in sharing your faith. Then think about what good things might happen if you told more people about the love and grace of Jesus. Isn't it worth the risk to increase your commitment to fulfill the mission of Jesus?

Personal Action

In this chapter of *The Story* we are called to avoid being shaped into the image of the world and its patterns. Identify one way you are letting the world squeeze you into its mold and commit to break free. You might even want to contact a member of your small group this week and ask them to pray for you and keep you accountable in this area.

Read for Next Session

Take time before your next small group to read chapter 30 of *The Story.*

SESSION 30

Paul's Final Days

Becoming like Jesus takes a lifetime . . .
and then some.

Introduction

Picture a mother teaching her son to eat. The mother is patient and kind; the son is throwing a fuss.

"Here you go, Honey; you can hold the spoon and scoop up the corn all by yourself. Like this . . ." The mother holds her own spoon, scoops up some corn, and puts it in her mouth in an effort to show her son how it is done. As Mom eats she says, "This is delicious; using a spoon is fun!"

Her son shakes his head vigorously. "No! You feed me!" A minute later, he throws the spoon on the floor. "Feed me, Mommy, feed me!" he cries.

Exasperated, the mother slides her chair a little closer to her son and looks right into his teary eyes. "Sweetie," she says, "you are a big boy, perfectly healthy; you should be feeding yourself. You're twenty-three years old."

Now stop and ask yourself, "What would I think if I saw this drama unfold in real life?" The idea of a mother spoon-feeding a healthy, grown young man just because he does not want to do it himself seems unthinkable.

Sadly, this happens all too often in our spiritual lives and the church. God longs to see us mature, to go deeper in our faith. If we are not careful, we can become content with where we are and forget God's call for us to grow, more and more, into people who live and look like Jesus.

Talk About It

Tell about a time in your spiritual journey when you felt God call you to a new level of commitment and growth in your faith. How did you respond to this call?

DVD Teaching Notes

As you watch the video segment for session 30, use the following outline to record anything that stands out to you.

Paul pens "the Prison Epistles"

Paul passes the baton to Timothy

Timothy stands up for his beliefs

Becoming a part of the new community called the church

DVD Discussion

1. Randy told a wonderful little story about a sculptor chiseling away everything that did not look like a lion. What is one area in your life that God is "chiseling" and how is he calling you to partner with him in this sculpting project?

> *Our prayer needs to be that God would chisel away everything in our lives that doesn't look like Christ.*

2. As the apostle Paul drew near the end of his life, he expressed some thoughts about how he had lived; how he had served God with humility, faithfully proclaimed the truth, called Jews and Gentiles to repentance, and bravely faced prison and other hardships. As you think about how you will invest the rest of your life, name one thing you really want to do for Jesus and one step you can take to move closer to this goal.

3. While under house arrest in Rome, Paul wrote a letter (an epistle) to the believers in Ephesus. In it he lifted up a beautiful, powerful prayer (Ephesians 1:16 – 23; *The Story*, p. 453). What are some elements of this prayer and what can we learn about prayer from Paul's example?

4. What "before Jesus" and "after Jesus" pictures did Paul paint of the Ephesian believers (Ephesians 2; *The Story*, pp. 453–454)?

   Tell about one big contrast people would see if they could watch a twenty-four-hour video surveillance tape of your life before you trusted Jesus as Savior compared to who you are today.

5. God cares greatly about unity among Christians. The apostle Paul gave several examples of our call to oneness (Ephesians 4:4–6; *The Story*, p. 455). What are they and how can our unity around these "ones" strengthen the church and become a witness to the world?

> *We need to grow. We need day by day to become more like Christ. As we do, others will be able to see Christ in us and through us and just might decide to follow him too. There is no greater calling.*

6. Faith lived out within the family is another great concern to God. What is one practical lesson you learned from Paul's teaching on family relationships (Ephesians 5:21–6:4; *The Story*, p. 455) and how might you live out that truth on a regular basis?

7. Beyond faith in our literal home, we have a larger Christian family. Just as Paul was a spiritual father to Timothy, we can enter relationships like this among the family of God. Tell about a spiritual parent of yours and how God has used this person to shape your faith. Then tell about a person God has allowed to be your spiritual child and how you are seeking to help him or her grow into maturity in Christ.

8. Paul celebrated the fact that Timothy had known the Scriptures from his youngest days because of a rich spiritual heritage of faith in his birth family. How can we make our homes a place of spiritual growth and health? (Perhaps you might use *The Story* as a family reading resource.)

---

9. Read movements 1 and 5 of *The Story* (pp. 10–11 of this participant's guide). It all begins in a garden and it all ends in perfect paradise. What does this teach us about God's desire to be in relationship with us?

Closing Prayer

As you take time to pray, here are some ideas to get you started:

- Thank God for the spiritual parents he has placed in your life.
- Ask for the Spirit to use you in the lives of the spiritual children he has given you.
- Surrender your heart and life to God and invite him to chisel away anything that needs to be removed from your life so that you can become more and more like Jesus.

Between Sessions

Personal Reflections

In his second letter to Timothy, the apostle Paul used three images — soldier, athlete, and farmer — to paint a picture of how we are to live as believers (2 Timothy 2:1 – 7; *The Story*, p. 457). In the coming week, read about these three examples and reflect on how you might learn from them.

Personal Action

If you have a person in your life who has been a spiritual parent, write them a letter or give them a call to communicate how much they mean to you and how God has used them to help you walk with Jesus. If you have a person whom God is calling you to influence as a spiritual parent, make time in the coming weeks to connect with this person, continue to invest in their life, cheer them on, and be part of God's process of chiseling away anything that does not look like Jesus.

Read for Next Session

Take time before your next small group to read chapter 31 of *The Story.*

SESSION 31

The End of Time

God wins!
If we are on his side,
we win too.

Introduction

For many years, popular radio personality Paul Harvey would tell stories about real-life people and situations. With his soothing voice, perfectly suited for radio, he would spin every tale with great detail. Each story ended with a surprising twist followed by Harvey's signature line, "And now you know the rest of the story!"

There was something very gratifying about gaining fresh new insight that helped you put together the pieces of a story you thought you already knew.

Such is the case when we read chapter 31, the book of Revelation, which gives us insight to how God's story ends ... and how eternity begins. With beautiful portrayals of Jesus, clear teaching for the church, and vivid word pictures of the end of time, John wrote down what he saw and heard in a great vision. As we are drawn in by the drama, we gain the fresh hope that comes when we realize that God wins. We are inspired to stand strong until all of this becomes a reality ... and we know it will.

If we listen closely to *The Story*'s final words, it's almost as if we can hear the silky tones of Paul Harvey's voice saying, "And now you know the rest of the story!"

Talk About It

Tell about the ending of one of your favorite books or children's stories. Why do you like this ending?

DVD Teaching Notes

As you watch the video segment for session 31, use the following outline to record anything that stands out to you.

John's vision

No more tears

"Trees of life"

God's Upper Story vision is completely restored

DVD Discussion

1. John painted an amazing picture of Jesus (Revelation 1; *The Story*, pp. 459 – 461). According to this portrait, who is Jesus and what has he done?

2. The book of Revelation includes short letters written to seven real churches in the ancient world. What did Jesus' letter to the church in Ephesus (Revelation 2:1 – 7; *The Story*, p. 461) say regarding the following:
   - What they were doing well
   - Where they needed to grow or change
   - What action they should take

   What are specific ways we can make sure that Jesus remains the first love of our life and the first love in the life of the local church?

3. In his letter to the church in Laodicia (Revelation 3:14 – 21; *The Story*, p. 462) Jesus told the people he did not want them to be "lukewarm." What does it look like when the church becomes lukewarm and what can we do to make sure our church stays hot for God?

4. In John's vision, he got glimpses of heavenly worship (Revelation 4 – 5; *The Story*, pp. 463 – 465). What from these scenes do you learn about worship and how might this shape the way we engage and enter into praise of our God?

5. It is a serious and sobering reality that all people will spend eternity in heaven or hell. How does the book of Revelation affirm this reality and how should this spur us to share the message and love of Jesus with the people in our life?

6. John offered us a vision of what heaven will be like (Revelation 21:1 – 22:5; *The Story*, pp. 467 – 469). What specific element of this vision makes you excited to spend eternity in this glorious place?

> *Revelation, the last book of the Bible, has sparked so much hope in believers throughout the ages. It keeps us going in the darkest of times. Regardless of how difficult life may be in the moment, we have, through Christ's sacrifice, this wonderful place to look forward to.*

7. In the DVD segment, Randy talked about how the hope of heaven touches his heart because he knows he will see his mom again, and they can worship Jesus together. Name one person you love who is already with Jesus. How does the hope of seeing this person again make heaven even more wonderful?

8. The end of *The Story* is this: God will be with his people again. This has been his goal from chapter 1 to chapter 31. This life is really a time to practice for heaven. What can you do on a daily basis to stay close to God and have a dynamic friendship with him?

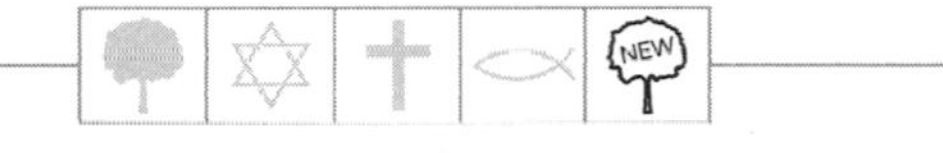

9. Read movement 5 of *The Story* (p. 11 of this participant's guide). How does the reality and hope of heaven inspire you to share God's story and your story?

> *The Story comes to an end.*
> *But it's really the beginning.*

Closing Prayer

As you take time to pray, here are some ideas to get you started:

- Celebrate the glory and majesty of Jesus, the First and Last, the Alpha and Omega, the Lamb of God slain before the foundation of the world.
- Thank God that you know the rest of the story and that you are confident that God wins!
- Pray for power to stand strong in faith until the end of the story is experienced.

In the Coming Days

Personal Reflections

Think back over your journey through *The Story* and reflect on all you have learned. You might want to look back over any notes you have jotted down in this participant's guide or your copy of *The Story.* Thank God, over and over again, for his loving persistence with us human beings!

Personal Action

Find a small group of believers (or nonbelievers) who don't really know the big story — the flow of the Bible — and offer to lead them through a study of *The Story.* As you have learned to see the big picture of God's love and activity in human history, share this gift with others.

PRODUCTS AVAILABLE FOR THE STORY

The Story Children's Curriculum

The Story:
Preschool Curriculum
Ages 2-5

The Story:
Early Elementary Curriculum
Ages 4-8

The Story:
Elementary Curriculum
Ages 9-12

This new, multilevel curriculum is based on the thirty-one stories found in the children's versions of *The Story*. The preschool level is parallel to *The Story for Little Ones*; the early elementary level corresponds with *The Story for Children*; and the elementary level corresponds with *The Story for Kids*. The engaging lessons are formatted around relatable Scripture references, memory verses, and Bible themes. Small and large groups will enjoy the hands-on, age-appropriate activities. All materials are available on CD or as a download.

The Story Trading Cards

The Story Trading Cards:
Preschool

The Story Trading Cards:
Elementary

These packs of trading cards are created to correspond with *The Story* curriculum for children or can be used on their own. Designed to help with Scripture memorization, each card depicts a scene or character from the Bible with a Bible verse and important facts. Each pack contains thirty-one cards. Card size: 2.5" x 3.5"

Share Your Thoughts

With the Author: Your comments will be forwarded to the author when you send them to *zauthor@zondervan.com.*

With Zondervan: Submit your review of this book by writing to *zreview@zondervan.com.*

Free Online Resources at

www.zondervan.com

Zondervan AuthorTracker: Be notified whenever your favorite authors publish new books, go on tour, or post an update about what's happening in their lives at www.zondervan.com/authortracker.

Daily Bible Verses and Devotions: Enrich your life with daily Bible verses or devotions that help you start every morning focused on God. Visit www.zondervan.com/newsletters.

Free Email Publications: Sign up for newsletters on Christian living, academic resources, church ministry, fiction, children's resources, and more. Visit www.zondervan.com/newsletters.

Zondervan Bible Search: Find and compare Bible passages in a variety of translations at www.zondervanbiblesearch.com.

Other Benefits: Register yourself to receive online benefits like coupons and special offers, or to participate in research.